Seeing Things:
A Chronicle of
Surprises

Seeing Things: A Chronicle of Surprises

Richard A. Hawley

Walker and Company
New York

First published in the United States of America in 1987 by the Walker Publishing Company, Inc.

Book design by Irwin Wolf & Laurie McBarnette
Jacket drawing by M. W. Hawley

Library of Congress Cataloging-in-Publication Data

Hawley, Richard A.
    Seeing things.

    Summary: The author writes of his growing up in the Midwest just after World War II.
    1. Hawley, Richard A.—Biography. 2. Authors, American—20th century—Biography. 3. Middle West—Social life and customs. [L. Hawley, Richard A. 2. Authors, American. 3. Middle West—Social life and customs] I. Title.
PS3558.A8236Z477   1987   813'.54 [B] [92]   87-10614
ISBN 0-8027-0987-7

Printed in the United States of America

10 9 8 7 6 5 4 3 2 1

For David

. . . *One muddles through the years for the sake of those one or two moments which are indisputedly great. Though such moments can occur on the battle field, in a cathedral, at the summit of a mountain, or during storms at sea, they are experienced more frequently at a bedside, on the beach, in moldy courts of law, or while driving down sun-warmed macadam roads on inauspicious summer afternoons: for the castles of the modern age are divided into very small rooms.*

—Mark Helprin, *Winter's Tale*

Seeing Things:
A Chronicle of
Surprises

Introduction:
The Road to
Emmaus

The man who does not believe that each day contains an earlier, more sacred and auroral hour than he has yet profaned has despaired of life, and is pursuing a descending and darkening way.

—Henry David Thoreau, *Walden*

Even apart from the particular things he had to say, Thoreau was a remarkable writer. He asked, and set out to answer, the biggest question: if you *really* look, what is there to see? Like a child, he wanted to know the truth and could not have been more direct in pursuing it. He went *right* at it—not into "nature"; anybody can do that, but into nature *after* it. He could get almost shrill talking about it: how of all the things that occur to one in reflection, of all the things we say to each other, and of all the things that are printed of

1

human affairs—troop movements, wafery increments of diplomacy, the devastating house fire, the latest instance of a primal crime—so few speak to our deepest knowing or needs.

To the extent we learn to converse in the lame language of the News, we kill ourselves a little, diminish ourselves. And for what? For the wan illusion of an easy, reliable Real World? The world where there is always "too much month left at the end of the money," where cars and refrigerators are not what they were when somebody was young, where a little civic initiative would clean up the streets, turn empty-eyed youth away from drugs, defuse the unthinkable bombs?

There is nothing in the News—or if there is, if the real thing should erupt through the banality of a standard medium, then the very idea of News makes way before it like debris before the wind. The real thing: what newsperson is even trying to figure it out?

The real thing. A friend of mine, an Englishman, has just returned to me the diaries of C. S. Lewis's brother, Warren. "They were perfect," he said. "Exactly what I like. College rooms and country pubs, a lot of getting wet and cold, then coming in before a roaring fire for a whiskey."

My friend is an honest reader; this is exactly what Warren Lewis's journals are about—and nothing could be less commonplace. And this summer, on a sunny, jewel-clear day on Cape Cod, a distinguished old gentleman, my wife's uncle, emerged dripping from the harbor after his twice-daily swim and joined me on the float. He is eighty and nearly blind. As he spread himself out next to me on the warm planks, he said with great feeling, "I *don't* know which I like more, getting wet or getting dry." The same thing, the real thing, artlessly said.

Enduringly great writers of course do the same thing, in

a rather more sustained, practiced way. Their gift is to portray a complete and vivid world, both new and familiar, as knowable as the waking world, only closer to what is most urgent, and lacking the very things which, deadeningly, take up all our time. It is a wonder that one can sense and respond to the real fictional thing, yet keep our waking distance from it, unconsciously afraid of it. From sad, safe distances, readers are apt to allow themselves an occasional, perhaps even overwhelming "intimation" before retreating into banality. But insistent voices draw us out again, remind us. Lewis shares his "northern-ness," his joy. Kenneth Grahame's Rat and Mole, transfixed before the Piper at the Gates of Dawn, show us where we belong: where we actually are, if we have the courage to surrender to it.

Consider the life of Christ for story value: the real thing made flesh, made man—historical, concrete, particular. He lived precisely *there* and *then,* was placed in family, in faith, in a political jurisdiction, in culture. We know about as much about him as we know about Alexander, Cleopatra, and Caesar Augustus, although we tend to find Christ increasingly elusive, and them increasingly like us.

Speaking personally, although I have the gospel narratives fixed fairly clearly in mind and know most of his spoken words by heart, Jesus has not grown in the least familiar. Is it something in the narrative style that makes him seem so ordinary on the cross? Resurrected, why was he so hard to recognize? Then so easy to recognize?

He supposedly walked for hours with disciples on the road to Emmaus before they recognized him in resurrected form. But perhaps every one of us is on a kind of road to Emmaus, not looking carefully, not quite remembering. Some might snap out of it, behold the truth, and become renewed in the Presence. Some continue on their way, too full of a future, of Emmaus, of all the news to come. The former are a little hard to believe; they seem to speak in myths. The latter are more credible, but their news is a little deadening, like history.

But the real thing, the kind of experience Thoreau set out to find, seems to peep out of both myth and history, elusive as a fragment of a dream suddenly recalled. One can make a life out of ignoring the real thing, but it is hard to imagine a life in which the real thing does not periodically *present* itself. How futile to dismiss it when it does, to explain it away. It is better—and always surprising—to go after it, to stalk it like a deer.

The following is an account of such a search, my own, and what I found was the very last thing I expected.

R. A. H.
Marion, Massachusetts
Summer 1986

4

Advent

The first thing I remember is Christmas. For once, everything came together and made sense. The people—my bright-toothed mother, my dark-animal father, and a shadowy sister—now formed a relationship to one another, and to me. They were all of them in anticipation of something. They were happy and assumed me into their happiness. It involved a spangled, pine-sweet tree in the parlor (visible, when the door was open, through the bars of the crib). Christmas was out there around and about that tree, shimmering in laughter, surprise, bright colors, and pine scent, and I was lifted up and carried out into it.

The tree in the parlor was more recollection than discovery. Snow on the boughs of a fir tree—peach-colored in dawn light, smoky blue in afternoon light—has always been absolutely right. Is there anything more achingly sweet and settled and old? Taken inside, the tree's secret is kept and stored in glittering strips of foil, reflecting glass balls, crystal-line snowflakes, straw dwarves, delicate china deer, little gilded bells, all kept gently aflame with a spray of electrified gems. The darker the room, the quieter and more beckoning the light. I recognized it then, just as surely as my daughters recognize it now.

Outside, in winter, the secret is all in the light. Every-where we look we are drawn after light that has always just departed. Inside, the secret is in light captured: in fire. The fireplace blaze or the rose-blue coals later *are* sentimental (sentiment is captured grace), but they are more than that; they are reminders. So is every candle. So, too, the lights on a tree. Even the desk lamp, the floor lamp across the room are reminders—provided they are *seen* as lights; that is, instances of light against darkness. But ordinary light—the overhead fixtures that whiten the whole room—negate, erase everything. (Perhaps nothing more than good, standard, up-to-code lighting has barred us from the numinous.) The more captured the light, the better. Through a glass darkly gives a twinge. But through a *colored* glass produces genuine long-ing: through a jeweled facet, through stained glass, through a glass of amber sherry, through burgundy, through clear beer in a pilsner.

It was in the softest captured light, in the remote gold of candles from the apse of a stone church, that I first heard the Christmas story. Does one "hear" it or "receive" it? "Join" it is better—"rejoin" it still better. The words were St. Luke's, and the minister's voice was deep and reedy and sure, a good instrument for Luke.

> And it came to pass in those days,
> that there went out a decree
> from Caesar Augustus, that all
> the world should be taxed . . .

In the center of the apse and surrounded by candles was a nativity creche. It fuses in my memory with the small creche we would set out on white cotton over our mantelpiece at home. In each—and perhaps in every nativity creche in the world—the light falls from above the kneeling and attending figures, the peripheral ones in silhouette, only the infant Jesus fully illuminated. Everything beyond the nativity is pure night, where in fact I was in the dark of my pew, beholding, from a vantage point somewhat farther off than the shepherds abiding in the fields. There, in the church on Christmas eve, I became conscious for the first time of how fear and longing can combine, can be appropriate responses to the same thing. I am sure every child at the nativity understands the shepherds perfectly. When in the still night the angel of the Lord comes upon them, they are sore afraid as well as pierced through with desire. A carol has only to set the scene.

A similar soft light, the preserved light of a log fire, captured further in the heavy brass of the fireplace implements, would signal from my grandparents' living room throughout the late, dark Christmas afternoon. Full from dinner, everyone stretched out in armchairs or, like me, reclining close to the fire on the carpet, we simply listened for it and basked in it. As likely as not, snow fell outside. This was not a re-created "Victorian" scene. Although the Victorians perhaps first assembled it and formalized it, they did not invent it, as some loveless speculators have claimed. Others have needed it, found it, and given it form. We continue to need it and sometimes to find it. Dickens helps. Keats (in "The Eve. of St. Agnes") helps. Dylan Thomas helps.

It is easy to find, and practically all of us find it in some guise or other. But just as it seems we are about to be transformed by it, we spoil it. Each of us becomes, helplessly, Scrooge in reverse. By age six we may have lost the

7

best of it. I did. Just as surely as Christmas is about desire, as soon as one becomes self-conscious of the desire, the first thing one does is to direct it to inherently unsatisfying objects: presents, tastes and smells, the *form* of the festivities. These things are of course easily comprehensible to a child, and because on a practical, everyday level such things are desirable, they replace the original and ultimate mystery of Christmas. But this substitution of desires is hopeless. The real beauty of presents and of other occasional delights at Christmastime is their inexplicable bounty. Lucky children may one morning experience an intimation of *infinite* bounty, provided by an all-seeing provider who, magically, *knows what we want*. As soon as we are able to be shrewd and sensible and clear about what we want in the way of delight, we are at once and forever aware of the finitude of the world's bounty. We become acquisitive. We learn where the bounty comes from, and we begin to help provide it, aware of what everything costs. We may continue to feel intensely at Christmastime, but not for Christmas. We are, if we are honest, let down, may even feel duped. The ultimate weariness, the ultimate sadness in response to this early mistake is to damn the holiday for having become so "commercial."

By the time I was seven, Christmas had become too commercial for me. A set of blue perfume bottles in a gift box caught my eye in the drugstore, and I stole it for my mother for Christmas. Seven is not so young as you think. I knew exactly what I was doing. I picked up the box as if casually inspecting it. I looked around. I feigned nonchalance. I did not even let *myself* see my right hand slip the box under my coat. I walked out of that store's saffrons and reds and blues, out of its clinking and chatter and recorded carols, into the cold, dark street and headed home. I got away with that theft and felt only a deadened apprehension—a blocked feeling rather than a feeling—when my mother opened the package on Christmas morning and showed her kind surprise.

It was, I am sure, in July of the following year that I had the most colorful and powerful dream of my life; it was awful. I had spent the day of the dream with a friend constructing a shanty "fort" out of scrap lumber at the back of our garage. The dream began as I stepped out of the dinginess of this shelter into such brilliant sunshine that the blue of the sky seemed charged through with whiteness. The sky somehow made it clear that everything was over for me on earth. I began to feel both sad and terrified. Then the sky filled with song: "Hark the Herald." The voices were women's, and the chorus was overpowering in its beauty. At the word "angel" in the carol, a formation of angels—all in luminous rainbow-striped robes—came floating over our house and down over the garage roof toward me. I gave myself up to them, reaching, as an infant reaches to be picked up by his mother; I died. Next I was in a white marble court up in the glass-blue heaven. Rainbow-robed men, no longer anonymous angels but bearded patriarchs along the lines of those illustrated in my Sunday school books, were deliberating about me. Suddenly, horribly, a great trap door was pulled up from the marble floor, revealing what I knew was a bottomless pool of bubbling pumpkin-colored swill: excrement and vomit. From somewhere above, the perfectly rigid form of my neighbor friend, the boy who had helped me build the fort, was lowered feet first into the swill. I could see him, seemed to be with him, as he went under. He was to drown, an appalling endless drowning. Whole thoughts, whole sentences rose to consciousness: *you could die, you could really die*, and *dying is not the end*. Now I was poised and rigid above the pool, my eyes turned up to the solemn, beautifully robed patriarchs and, above them, the inexpressibly splended blue of the heavens.

9

I awoke from that dream profoundly and unsentimentally aware of my own mortality. The dream, even when it was horrible, was beautiful. Certain paintings take me back to it, especially the blue pigment medieval artists used to illuminate skies in their books of hours, a color—glass blue—almost standard in the skies of classical painters to follow. The rainbow-striped robes I now know to be the robes of some of the creche figures in our mantelpiece nativity scene.

My theft, my dream, and now my every appetite propelled me out of the sweet joy of early Christmas. Mortal now, and possibly damned, I began to make my own way.

History

I was five or six when calendar years began to have meaning for me, and the first year of history that conveyed meaning to me was 1945. 1945 seemed portentous for two reasons: it was the year I was born, and it was the year World War II ended. The termination of the war and my birth have always seemed to me intimately linked events. As I saw it, my birth had somehow hastened the cessation of hostilities and chaos, as if my appearance, in poorish condition in a badly run wartime hospital in Chicago, said in effect to the world, "All right, clear all of this up: Richard and his whole story require a different kind of setup." Even now my birthday arouses agreeable feelings of awful things being over. As it happened, in 1945, the end of the war brought my father back from the Pacific to my mother, my sister, and me, and in a true sense "awful things were over" for our family, and a new story did begin for us.

I both could and could not understand World War II. When my father was sent overseas, my mother, pregnant with me, and my infant sister moved in with my grandparents. Then and for years afterward, my grandparents' house was Order and Art. The rooms were settled and ancient: marvelous and richly colored designs of the china plates showed up through the food. On the mantel, on shelves, inside glass cabinets were china figurines: dancers, shepherd girls, goats, horses. In dusky pictures framed in old gold were shadowy country lanes down which farmers led flocks of sheep away from the viewer toward a rosy and darkening horizon.

The house was full of *things*. My grandfather was a hobbyist, and there were endless objects to engage the youthful eye: grotesquely, wonderfully shaped faces in the ceramic, pewter-lidded beer mugs lining the shelves, a circular rack of elaborately carved pipes, rich leather volumes of his stamp collections—the intricate engraving and the apricot, green, rose, and blue inks of which fixed in my mind an enduringly lovely notion of "foreign." In an old trunk in the cellar was a velvet-lined box of small, highly polished pistols: real ones, a boy's dream.

Inside and, especially, out, the house was always in a state of gentle transformation. Fruit trees were being installed, a house-encircling hedge, latticework over the side door. It seems the house was always being painted or repainted, but the colors were never the ordinary ones; instead there were dark rusty reds, creams, yellows, smoky blues.

But flowers were the house's glory. My grandmother knew all about bounty, about bush fullness, about ivy, about roses and lattice, about opulence and delicacy. In reflective, arid moments I think back and ask: was it really anything out of the ordinary? Doesn't every child see as much in every garden, in every stamp collection for that matter? Isn't all the wonder and fascination rather about oneself, a precious way of saying "I discovered my senses"? Perhaps—but there was something objectively and substantially true in it, too. This—the objective beauty of my grandparents' house—came as something of a surprise to me, and it was brought home in an unexpected way, years after I first sensed it.

Without question the most unsavory boy in our town was George Pennington. By the time he was ten he was known townwide for bullying girls, for stealing from stores, for throwing stones through glass, for the most offensive cursing. Twice he had ridden my bike home from school and no doubt would have kept it, had my father not stormed the Pennington's garage and brought it home. He was the first even remote peer I knew who smoked. His standard turnout was a pair of blue jeans worn low on the hip, held there by a thick black belt buckled at the side. In the warmer months, when he was most visible, he wore a plain white T-shirt, the short sleeves of which were rolled up over his scrawny shoulders. His oily hair was slicked straight back. A bad boy. George Pennington would sometimes follow me around. He liked me. One afternoon, as I lay for some reason at the inside base of my grandparents' hedge, I observed George Pennington and a companion bicycling lazily up the street in my direction. They stopped their bikes at the curb in front of the house and exchanged a comment or two. George squinted and looked around, perhaps for me. After a pause, he said, with moving conviction, "Now *that's* a beautiful place," looked on for a minute longer, and pedaled off. It *was* a beautiful place, a modest house in a modest residential neighborhood, complicated as patchwork, a little surprising, but just, surprisingly, right.

My grandmother was English, from Portsmouth, and her people, my cousins, still live in a rolling Hampshire village some miles inland from there. In consequence of a great and very youthful romance with a wounded American soldier she was tending during the First World War, she decided to emigrate to the States—to Chicago—to marry him. This was the Chicago of Carl Sandburg—builder of railroads, stacker of wheat—it was also the Chicago of Al Capone, gangland, and jazz. There was something powerful and mechanized about it even then. It was cold, too, and sooty, all out of scale with Portsmouth, the sea, and the Hampshire hills.

As it happened, my grandmother's American was a German—a Breitsprecher. His people stood for order and plain speaking. He was a man for whom events followed one another with the reassuring regularity of liturgy: a time for listening to the Victrola, a time to clean one's pipes, a time to paint in oils, a time to attend to the stamps. Meals—even tea, which was served with a British flourish—were magnificent. In that rich, mysterious household my grandparents tended one another with what seemed to me adoration, addressed each other only with endearments, which was somehow not incongruous with my grandfather's stern, rather Jehovan manner of address. "There was love in that house," my grandmother liked to pronounce after my grandfather died. There was. There was love, and there was order. More than that there was, as in Dante's paradise, hierarchies and systems of order, order in each cupboard, order in each drawer, Hampshire and Bavaria fused and transported to Chicagoland.

In 1945 the war was over. I awakened into a world where England was married to Germany, and all was teeming and blooming.

Souls

But back at our house something was wrong. There were dark places in the house. There were rats in the alley. My sister Binky not only sensed the wrongness, but she also lived it. One of my earliest memories is looking up from my blanket on the living room floor at my sister who lay heavily swaddled and reeking of the mentholated rubs applied to her chest, back, and throat to ease her bronchitis. She was not eased. Her cough rasped and honked with a terrible regularity. It sounded to me as if she must be scraping herself raw. Through all of it her face was eerily vacant. She had a look, and one could catch glimpses of it all through her foreshortened life, of bottomless disappointment: not quite disappointment—an *acknowledgment,* rather, that some central element in life, some prize or blessing, had been denied her and would never be offered. She could convey the kind of

15

profound sadness, bordering on terror, that one is more likely to see in the faces of the unhappy elderly.

Not that my sister moped around. To the contrary, nobody ever willed love and cheer more mightily. A petite little girl—she grew up to be just under five feet—she was barely acknowledged in school, although she quietly bred great passions and loyalties for other children and to her teachers. Binky would open up like a flower to praise, but very little of it came her way. She was always a little too small for what was going on. Her triumphs, like riding a bicycle or learning to dive, were usually passé to her peers by the time she mastered them. Some things she could not learn: mathematics, in particular. Algebra? How did it relate to one's personal longings? To *The Wind in the Willows*? To animals? Why *do* these things to *X*? Some things she perhaps could learn but did not: geography, history, politics. Europe's relationship to Asia was unclear to her. The events between biblical times and Hitler were radically compressed; she saw those years as more or less similar, their monuments and costumes and leading characters assuming a generalized "old-fashioned" aura. Omaha, she believed, was a state.

But in compensation she knew animals. She did not know *about* animals; she knew *them*. There was a special affinity for the statuesque: wild horses, deer, wolves, foxes, tigers, lions, cheetahs, panthers, most dogs, and all cats. In my memory she never just "looked at" an animal; she met its eye. *You,* she would seem to say, *I understand*. Since our family was never more countrified than suburban, she had to make do with brief encounters in zoos, still briefer ones alongside a northern Michigan road in the course of a family vacation, and pictures in magazines. The pictures, like the Disney animal films she loved, probably helped to "romanticize" animals for her, but I am certain this carried her deeper

16

into, not father away from, the reality of animals. Each tethered horse spotted alongside the highway was an intimation of unspeakably beautifiul antecedents running free through the earth's vernal parts. Every cat was a silent corner away from a moonlit forage about the ancient monuments of the Nile.

My sister's story is hurtful for me to recall even now. Its unexpectedly violent ending still catches me short, on the brink of a question I know will not be answered. By all the standard measures, nothing went right for my sister. Perhaps her story is best seen through the lives of her closest animals.

My sister owned three dogs in the course of her life, but a fourth, one that preceded her into the world, is probably the most important. My grandparents had a matronly, smoke-colored, long-haired dog named Susy. A big animal, Susy had a worried, intelligent-looking face. Her breed was always referred to as part German shepherd, but she bore no physical resemblance, except perhaps in size, to any German shepherd I have seen.

Susy was famous in the family for her ability to baby-sit for us in my grandparents' back lawn. Even as infants, my sister and I could be left with her on a blanket in the yard. If we wriggled off the blanket, Susy would nose us back on. No intruder, dog or human, could enter the yard without an unnerving showdown with Susy, lips drawn back over her teeth, tensed, ready to rip. Otherwise, the photographs suggest, she was pleased to lie watchfully at the blanket's edge, in a way impossible to describe, *related* to us in the blanching sunlight. When I grew old enough to be more fully aware of her, Susy impressed me as the most reliable *adult* in any assembled company. She never seemed to do an irritable or self-regarding thing. When we got big enough to think it would be fun to ride her as though she were a horse, she would wait until we had mounted, then gently sit on her

17

haunches so we would slide furrily down to the floor. Occasionally my grandmother would scold us: "You're going to hurt that dog. You're going to break her back!"

Around the fire on winter afternoons, Susy was a matchless head cushion, exuding her own warmth and a faint scent. One dozed more easily, I think, resting on her flank and hearing her heart working deep and muffled inside her. Occasionally, after days out of the dog's presence, my sister would rise out of a distraction and pronounce, "I love Susy." "Wonder dogs" of story—Lassie, Rin Tin Tin—would never for an instant strain my sister's credibility.

The first dog my parents bought for my sister turned out, perhaps inevitably, to be of a different spiritual order from Susy. It was a short-haired, inky-black puppy, eager and fidgety. Its breed was referred to as part cocker spaniel. My main recollection of its brief life with us was the extreme difficulty of getting it into my hands and arms. My sister named it Button.

My sister had only slightly better luck than I in gathering Button into her arms, but she was devoted to the dog nonetheless. Convinced, I now believe correctly, that this was in some essential but mysterious way, another instance of Susy, she adopted a course of observant patience with Button. She never considered accepting the general verdict that Button was, alternately, a "bad" and a "stupid" dog. My sister's perseverance in affection for an animal that could not be said to be responsive to her was remarkable in a four-year-old. Her love flowed directly outward to the animal; there was no demand on her part for Button to confirm what she wanted or what she was. The personal needs and self-love motivating so many "animal lovers" played no part in my sister's approach to Button. Such was the power of her conviction that the puppy's frantic scratchings, chewings, and boundings began to assume a fixed place in family life. There was going to be room, it appeared, even for this.

While still a puppy, Button was killed—run over by a car—one night when my father took him out for a walk before bed. We had just returned from an evening out, and as my sister and I were being tucked into bed, Button, more boundingly frantic than usual after his confined solitude, raced out the door ahead of my father and into the street. My mother informed my sister and me just after we had said our prayers. There was no precedent for such news. It only raised *questions*—and fear. My sister was inconsolable but not outraged. She seemed to recognize something: so *this* is the kind of life it is. Animal exuberance led straight into the world's deadly traffic: the untold, and perhaps the last, chapter of natural history. There was, I recall, an interminable night to think about it in the dark.

My sister's next real dog was preceded by a sudden and accidental pet, a black duck my father inadvertently won by tossing a wooden ring around its neck at a fair. He was at first bewildered by his prize, but we pleaded with him to keep it. We called it Blackie and took it home with us. For a day or two we chased the terrified bird around our darkened basement attempting to interest it in food. At length my sister became convinced that it belonged in nature; we had to let it go. It wouldn't do any good to let it go, my parents pointed out, since its wings had been clipped at the fair. Feeling troubled on Blackie's behalf, my sister somehow succeeded in getting it out from behind the furnace and outdoors.

Wings clipped or not, the duck could move quickly over sidewalk and lawn, faster than I could run. We tore after it down the block, frightened we might lose it, yet, for some reason, also giddy and thrilled. The distance between us and Blackie opened up farther and farther, and then, with a wonderful power, he glided up off the walk, over the telephone wires, up past the tree line and disappeared. With clipped wings? What did we know about clipped wings? The bird flew away, pulled up out of suburbia by some deep, avian knowing, but a knowing accessible to my sister.

After Button it never occurred to us that there would be another dog; they died. Nevertheless, one rainy spring evening the family dashed out of our car to the ticket window of a movie to find we were a half hour early. Next door was a pet shop and we ducked inside to get dry. The owner saw in my sister and me easy marks. "We've got some puppies— would you like to see them?" He handed my sister what looked like a ball of brown and white angora out of which protruded a foreshortened snout. My sister looked hard into its bright, moist eyes, then imploringly up to my parents. We asked what kind it was. The owner said, "Part border collie." There was no movie.

From the outset *this* dog was going to be a success. It liked us, thrilled and wriggled whenever someone woke up, came home, or entered a room. For reasons I cannot imagine now, we had difficulty determining its gender. Assuming first it was a female, my sister named it Cleopatra, "Cleo" for short. The name had just about become fixed through usage when, on the basis of some tentative anatomical research, we decided the dog was a male after all. Cast down a bit by this determination, my sister reluctantly renamed the dog "Chipper." "Chipper" stuck, even though a knowing neighbor soon afterward pronounced her a female, a fact confirmed later by two litters of puppies and never again questioned.

Chipper grew up into the most loving of dogs, in appearance a diminutive Susy, although perhaps less worldly-wise. She stayed close to my sister, physically close, through most of her school years, and jarring as those years were for my sister, I doubt that they would have been endured at all without Chipper, at her feet wherever she sat down, at the foot of her bed when she slept.

My sister had a miserable, wrenching time in school, and when she would come home feeling raw and overwhelmed, Chipper calmed her best, because she at least could not understand that school had diminished my sister. At school my sister did not matter, yet it required her attentive unease for most of the day, most of the year. In Chipper's unschooled eyes my sister was all that mattered. Binky knew better, but she was grateful for the affection all the same. Moreover, it was nearly enough.

As I have said, my sister was very petite. Nicely, delicately formed, she was always a decisive cut shorter than anybody else her age. This of course did not affect her much until there was an opportunity for comparison: school. From the very beginning, from the first day of kindergarten, she was not enough for school, not big enough, not tough enough, not shrewd enough. She was terrified by the noise, the crowds, the shoving. She was confused by instructions, afraid to speak out and perform for the only grown-up in the room, a woman, to whom, had it been allowed, she needed to cling until the fear and noise subsided.

After a few numbing weeks, she refused, miserably, to go any longer. There were terrible interludes by the front door in the morning, my mother buttoning up my sister's coat and reassuring her, as my sister shook in her clothes and cried in an urgent, rattling way, like a hurt animal. Urged out the door, she would not budge. For several days, she had to be walked to school One winter morning, she entered one school door and walked out another, returning home to find that my mother and I had gone out, leaving the house locked. Day closed in like night. There was no way in.

Chipper was not yet behind the door. I am told the bleating and the rhythmic banging of the hip into the front door went on for hours.

She had to go to school, and she did go to school. But there was a way out: she learned not to understand, to be impervious, profoundly unto herself. Her school reports improved; she was no longer a "problem."

Against the long line of Chipper's life—the ecstatic puppyhood, the adoringly watchful central years, and the stiffening, slowing period at the close—it is possible to chart my sister's coming of age. Since it had been painfully unacceptable to be "little," my sister, once she saw a clear pathway ahead, threw herself recklessly and fatally into being "big." Chipper had not been enough. The planned collie ranch she had envisioned as her life's work was no longer enough. The deep knowing of animals was very fine, but, she realized, useless in school and neighborhood.

For a year or two she immersed herself in movie magazines, poring over the faces of the most spectacularly successful women in the land of the "big." Out of that world she fashioned a physical image of herself that she would maintain until she died. The transformation of my sister into this dream image was uncompromising, radical. Everything had to change. Her brown hair was bleached to a nearly white shade of "blonde," then puffed and sprayed into an outsized "bouffant," the overall effect of which resembled more a futuristic mode of head gear than actual human hair. Beneath this finely spun silver globe, her features would also become transformed. I watched once as she painfully pulled the hairs out of her eyebrows with a tweezers, to make way for a pair of looping arches, sliver thin, penciled up over her brow onto her forehead. Onto her eyelashes were glued brushlike extensions which, combined with a moist dark line she painted around the whole of each eye, created a fascinat-

22

ing impression of complexity and weight. On special occasions other brilliant colorings, like those associated with tropical birds and fish, would appear between eye lid and brow. The rest of my sister's face, from the base of her neck to her hairline, was coated every morning with a flesh-colored batter she told me was a "base." Over the base she would apply various rouges and shadows until, despite metallic blond hair, she resembled an Oriental doll. The final touch was lipstick, always a "hot" shade of red or pink and always drawn up over the natural line of her upper lip.

My parents, particularly my father, regarded this transformation with clear disapproval. At his angriest, my father referred to my sister's hair and makeup as "phony." But from my sister's standpoint, what was real was "little," and was not enough.

I am now convinced that my sister's transformation was nothing more than a desperate desire at last finding form in the image of the female "stars" of the day. Because she intended to correct only herself, she was genuinely hurt and puzzled when the big world responded aggressively. My father's anger (and my teasing) were not the only responses. A distinctive type of young man—a "hood" in the standard parlance of the day—was aroused reflexively by the sight of my sister. "Hoods" began cruising their long, low rumbling cars along our street. Some made dates, entered the house. My sister sought only to please, but this was not possible given the dramatically opposed intentions of the hoods and my father.

Behind the ritual application of paints, oils, and sprays, my sister was coming undone. Her "appearance" (without which she did not feel substantial enough to go outside the house) gave offense. Her suitors, unbeckoned and unwanted for the most part, gave offense. The stylish, long-limbed beauties she could draw had no place in the high school's art classes. The show tunes she learned and sang in her room were not a part of the repertoire of the student chorus. Mathematical symbols swarmed around her like noise. The operation of machines, multistep instructions, college applications, job interviews—whoever *asked* for such complexities. My sister certainly did not. She wanted it to stop. When Chipper weakened and died an old dog's death, my sister lost all but the ornamental appreciation of animals.

Loosed from any reliable comfort, loosed from her good animal knowing, she thrashed about ineffectually in a world she really did not want and on terms she never agreed to. High school was somehow endured. A college was found and, after a year or so, abandoned. Clerical work was arranged for her in Chicago. The hoods had become young executives, and my sister accepted, without an instant's affection, one of them in marriage. All of this was long before I understood how apparently positive decisions are often made solely to *cut off possibilities.* The ultimate intimacy became for my sister the most unbearable violation of her self. Apart from her family—we did not understand her, but we knew her—she was suffocatingly alone. She reached out erratically for friendship. Late one night, tiny as she was, she broke through my grandmother's tightly bolted front door in a panic. "I had to see you!" she cried. "I've been wanting so much to die."

In a few years, after having a child by him, my sister left her husband. No one was surprised, but no one approved. Her daughter was a continuing marvel. Big, extroverted, tireless, she effortlessly took to, and was taken up by, the world of the big. This my sister viewed with wonder.

I will not draw this out. It became increasingly clear to my sister that she did not matter. She began to make eerie compensations. Elaborately ornate bric-a-brac began to appear in her little house: multitiered brass chandeliers tingling with glass pendants; china figurines; gold and silver candy boxes inlaid with bright stones; oil paintings framed in gold gilt; intricate clocks. Guided by destiny's sure hand, she responded on a whim—or as a last cry for help—to a newspaper advertisement for a dog. The dog, described as "part Husky," was physically striking. With the eyes of a doe and the appearance otherwise of an infinitely benign wolf, its long hair was pure white as it left the flesh, darkening at the extremities to silvers, grays, and blacks. The dog was "plush," and when my sister brought it home, it seemed a remarkable extension of the "plush" carpeting she had installed.

She called the dog Natasha, and it was apparent soon after she bought it that there was something seriously wrong with it. Large and outwardly healthy, the dog lacked even very basic motivation. It would eat if one led it by the collar to a dish, but not otherwise. It could not be house-trained. Moreover, it seemed acutely distressed whenever taken outdoors. If made to go out, Natasha would sit on her haunches on the nearest patch of green, whining and shivering, unmovable. Various diagnoses and verdicts were given of Natasha's condition, the most recurring being that she was "retarded." Whatever the case, no one proposed a remedy. Reclined on my sister's thick carpeting, she was a disquieting presence: far too big for the room, unnaturally calm, organically alive, but somehow dead. And there is no deadness so convincing as that conveyed by something technically alive. For a time conventionally "sorry for" the dog, my sister determined finally to get rid of it. The idea of my sister voluntarily giving up an animal was unsettling even to her. Calling on an executive ability rarely seen, she managed to find Natasha other lodging.

If we had thought about it more deeply at the time, my sister's giving up her dog would have been revealed as more than the "good sense" it appeared to be at the time. Good sense had *never* motivated my sister. She had loved animals and she had known them. The only positive projection she had ever made into adult life was her plan to breed collies on a remote, rural collie ranch. Had she *known* Natasha? If so, she must have known that unnerving deadness at her core. For someone who felt so inherently insubstantial as my sister did, Natasha's deadness may have seemed something of a confirmation. Getting rid of her may have been my sister's farewell.

As it happened, one unmanageable day, preceded by several barely endurable weeks, my sister arrived home late from the city. My parents protested. Didn't she realize there was a *baby* to look after? She realized. She realized that every foreseeable task, every likely prospect, every step taken upon waking, every breath drawn was pure will, pure effort. She realized she was not doing a good job. She did not know how to do a good job. Once there had been animals, but now animals had no souls. They were plush like the carpet, but not quite alive. A dog like that could not help. The makeup and glitter and bric-a-brac had not helped. Animals seemed so far away. She could no longer imagine a real one.

That evening, after an exchange of angry words with my parents, my sister drove home with her little girl and put her to bed. A few days earlier she had written me in England, where I was studying, telling me, among other things, that something oppressive was "following her around." That night when she was alone it caught up with her, and when it overcame her it was more than oppressive. It was more, even, than fear. It was I am sure, a summons from the very source of fear, shaming her, reminding her that she was not enough, that she had plainly never been enough.

She took an afghan my grandmother had given her and

went out into the garage, closed the doors, got into the car, and turned on the engine. Then she curled up on the seat and let the poison put her to sleep.

And so it would no longer be merely hypothetical to me that certain souls could behave more like "absences" than "presences." Souls in this condition constitute something like a negative charge in one's field of action. We are more likely to sense this as "something wrong" than to understand it, and the first impulse is to turn away. But we must not turn away from souls, not from any. Everybody, I have assured my sister thousands of times since her death, is enough.

An Intimation
In the Cellar

Our neighborhood in Chicago, until we left it for a suburb at the prairie's edge, was charged through with numinous presences. I have little doubt that most of the earth's surface is similarly charged. The more we rearrange that surface, and the faster we relocate ourselves over the rearrangements, the more insistent (and more incomprehensible) the numinous becomes. There was certainly nothing exotic on the surface of our residential street. We lived in a block of identical wooden row houses. The street connected at each end to busier arteries of traffic, and we were not far in any compass direction from warehouses, fields of scrap, trestles for the elevated trains—that specially desolate sort of wilderness found around the margin of large industrial cities.

Whatever had taken place along the great lake's rim before the row house, pocked pavement, oil drum, and trestle was incompletely stifled when I first opened my eyes to it. Tangles of green insisted on erupting behind sheds, along the foundations of the houses, in the cracks in the concrete walks: heavy, sour profusions of skunk cabbage, burdock, plantain. The narrow cinder alley that ran by our back gate was truer to the place than the paved street in front. In the alley everything was alive. Above all was the ancient urgency of animals. There were sinister gray and black rats glimpsed about the battered trash cans. These were not the agreeable long-haired country rats I would know later in the prairie and in *The Wind and the Willows*. These were large, swollen, smooth-flanked creatures, some of them the size of small dogs, wobbling mechanically as they made their way—until they were spotted. Then they slithered away, up over and under things, like reptiles. Cats, too, patrolled the alley, conveying always in their preoccupations an inherent importance. Dogs belonged in yards, not alleys, but occasionally a gangling mutt loose on a rove would pass amiably by, careering erratically from smell to smell.

The most focal hour of the week was the bright morning arrival of the garbage collector's horse and cart. In memory the horse's girth fills the alley, but that cannot have been true. The horse was the color of cinders and seemed to be pure weight. I was fascinated that all of its might was bound, with harness and traces of oily black leather, and that its eyes were blinded. Even so, this was the natural lord of the alley. I can see its great head against clear sky, the outline of its ears continuous with the rooftops of the houses across the alley. The man in the black vest and the black cap who tended the cart was also from another world—he was unimaginable clopping down the street in *front* of the house. He might have plied his trade in the same manner in a medieval burg. He might have been a gypsy, moving through a system of alleyways connecting the whole preindustrial world. In the wake of that horse, I believe, *anything* could come down that alley.

Two of the most arresting things to come down it (although I did not see them do it) were a pair of great black turtles. My mother saw them first, with stupefaction, when she took out the morning trash. When I was allowed outside to see them (warned not to touch, as they might be snapping turtles), they were immobile in the center of our back walk, their lusterless black shells as alien to house, yard, and alley as something extraterrestrial. Their feet and heads were fully retracted. There was no communicating with them. Were they dead? I asked. No, I was told. This was the way with turtles. Amazing to me, these two visitors: great ceramic mounds, death-still but *alive* inside. For two days, whenever I could, I watched them with rapt attention. Once while I was alone in the yard one of them moved a little, and I shrieked. The next morning they were gone, not a little at a time but all at once, completely gone. What else, I wonder, was periodically generated from alley and moved earth in the heart of that city? Deer and racoon and skunk fled to the green marge, but the more reptilian possum lingered in the rubble and refuse behind the garages. Rats, of course. But perhaps here and there, like our turtles, an eagle would materialize—or a sinewy lynx or, up out of the parched weeds, the puffed arrow head of a rattler.

There were mysteries inside the house as well. In the cellar, a dark place used only to store coal in a bin, entered only to check pipes and meters, a previous tenant had left a ruined upright piano. Hammers, felts, and wires were exposed. On this instrument I played my first musical notes, and their effect on me was at once transforming. We hear so many of them and in such lurid combinations, that it is easy to forget the wonderful clarity of a single sustained tone. I attended to several one damp morning in our cellar. I felt I

31

had discovered for mankind not only the tones, but also the ancient device that produced them. I tried notes in combinations, "thirds" and "fourths," and heard the foundations of harmony itself. Plucking and strumming the wires also produced the tones, but in different colors, in shivering metallics. I wanted simultaneously to bound up the steps and tell someone and to continue striking the tones; I could not leave the instrument. Discoveries like this were confined usually to dreams. This is exactly the kind of scene I would awaken out of, unable to return. I struck, plucked, strummed, and listened until my mother came down to fetch me. Somebody "explained" the piano, but the explanation did not fit. I have always visualized music as liquified colors. Chords are crystal. Progressions of chords are arrangements of crystals. That first musical morning in the cellar the surrounding dark was hung with crystals like stalactites in a cave. Trying to describe my discovery years later in poetry, I was accused by friends of being needlessly obscure.

> An uncertain child randoms through an old cold storage,
> Finds a bandy piano shivering in a shawl.

I learned actually to play the piano, by ear, before I was ten. Although initially rather eccentric in my fingering and in my key of preference (F sharp), I was harmonically true and could, within a few minutes, play anything I heard. I have played the piano with deep satisfaction ever since, for hours in succession if there is time. Piano playing is the only wholly engaging activity I know of that requires no effort. In fact, I cannot imagine playing by the will, *making* my fingers conform. Conversely, those who do not hear music in patterns and do not play by ear cannot imagine what it is like to do so. Occasionally a friend will ask, "How do you put all the parts of the song together like that?" sometimes followed by the dreaded "show me." The question is hard to answer. For a start I (and I assume other musicians who play by ear) don't *do* anything to the music, at least not initially. The first thing that happens when a tune engages attention or when it pushes to the fore in memory is that a visual pattern—a kind of grid—establishes itself, and in relation to that grid, the melody line and chords take their relative places; the crystals gather. No matter how novel or complex the music, it is necessarily a rearrangement of tones and chords already heard, played before, and stored. Every new piece is a rearrangement of parts of old ones. What one knows ("feels" is just as good a word for it) is what a tone *does* to another tone; the combinations, although endlessly delightful, are manageably finite. Considered this way a "song" is a (perhaps specially memorable) progression of single tones to which various things are done by other tones to shape and color it. I have said nothing about rhythm or cadence because, as I see it, rhythm is too elemental to discuss. Before we ever hear an identifiable rhythm, we have lived it: in the beating of our hearts, the right-left cadences of walking, etc. When we hear it, we have it. When it rouses us or, in the case of syncopation, surprises us, we know all there is to know about it.

Whether scored on a page or hanging in the air, songs present *possibilities* to the brain, possibilities to which one's fingers, more or less practiced, respond. I have learned what I felt to be irresistible music from scores, and I have learned it by ear; in each case, as elements begin to cohere, there is an undeniable experience of the music *being pulled through me* into being. I remember once tentatively working through one of the Bach Two-Part Inventions and feeling, as my fingers began to come alive, that I was no longer in control, but that the piece had taken over, was drawing itself ticklingly through me. To put it another way, I was an occasion

33

and a location for that particular piece, but I was not *making* it. The wonderful child's verse, one version of which goes

> The centipede was happy quite
> Until the mouse in fun
> Said, pray, which leg comes after which?
> Which threw the bug in such a twitch,
> It lay distracted in a ditch
> Considering how to run.

could not be truer of piano playing. I have more than once snapped out of a reverie while fingering through the teasing syncopations of, say, "Maple Leaf Rag," to stare at my whirring hands and consider exactly what they were doing—clunk, off the rails.

I am not sure, but I suspect that those who play instruments capable of producing different tones simultaneously—piano, guitar, harp, etc.—experience, even when playing in solitude, that rhapsodic, fluid *fit* of the sounds they are at that moment producing to what they most desire. It is lovely when it happens, and it happens, always, unexpectedly.

In the summer of my twentieth year I got a job (*job!*) playing the piano in the lounge of a great fortress of a lodge in Glacier National Park, Montana. The long glass front of the lounge looked out over the mottled peaks of the Continental Divide. Just sitting at that piano elevated me to an inner pitch of almost aching power and sweetness. Playing in that state, and occasionally playing well, was as close a communion with what is ultimate as I have felt—or can imagine feeling. For one thing, time is perceived altogether differently. There is a sense of its moving along in the old way, but the movement is framed in a larger, motionless perspective, beyond which I observed it with a pleasing lack of engagement. And, in the event anyone should wonder, the song played has a negligible effect on the quality of the

34

experience. Again, the song is just a progression of tones—although a distinctive, set progression—but the music grows more out of what is "done" to them than what has been scored into the progression's bare bones.

One night that summer I had a dream so powerfully charged, so clearly a *message,* that the waking experience that followed it seemed insubstantial for days. In the dream I looked downward from a great height at myself as I played a piano of brilliant crystal. I viewed myself from a high perch on the interior of a cylindrical tower, the crystal walls of which were faceted and flashing. The tower was tiered with rotating segments, perhaps floors of a hotel, and the rotations of each tier were independent of those of every other tier. The oblique facets of each crystal tier reflected the image of me playing the piano in such a way that in their dynamic multiplicity they created—in the manner of three-dimensional images projected by laser beams—a single image: me at the piano. The point—the message?—was that the working of the facets *was* me. They were also the song, Rodgers and Hart's "Where or When." From my perch I understood that the song had always been playing, but that nevertheless it somehow depended on me. There was a sense, but not a clear image, of a great crowd of faces, infinitely loving and infinitely hopeful that I would play. For although the song and I had already been "designed" and had been playing for eternity, there was an urgent sense of its being *about to begin.* Upon waking, I recall saying out loud, as "before" and "after" disengaged and zoomed to their waking poles, "Of course I'll play it." I said this, and still recall it, feeling inexpressible joy.

The Prairie and the Town

I don't think I have ever been to a small town in the United States that was not crying out for something. Taken together, the cries seem very sad and very sweet. The midwestern town where my family settled after we moved out of Chicago expressed a great ache. It was never clearer to me than on the hot, bright, Fourth of July morning when in addition to many other civic celebrations, the fire department demonstrated its capability by burning down a row of condemned frame houses near the village center. Each empty house, I recall, had a distinctive face, and each face expressed a decrepitude, a sadness, and a secret that would die with it in the fire.

> With the conviction of a house condemned,
> Each stood there drooping in the sun:
> Sad saloon from days of chicken coops,

Slender face, frail and peeling,
Empty windows staring dark—
It held its musty breath.

Gas was splashed about the halls,
The firemen trickled out the doors.
Captain Corbett lit the torch.
The house was dry. It grimaced once
And broke and buckled up in flames.

The mayor's speech was ready on the green.
The trumpets screamed, the bicycles
Rolled forward like kaleidoscopes.

The town was conceived in the days of chicken coops. Its founders had trickled out of Chicago's inhospitable commerce when the city itself was no more than a cow town. Or, diminished by a century of farming corn and wheat and dairy cows, they trickled in the direction of that commerce. This was before Chicago swallowed the town whole and all the towns around it. This was before the elms were razed, baring the new macadam and asphalt-shingled roofs to the baking July sun. This was when the village consisted of a half-timbered train station (dwarfed by elms, dappled by elms), and a cluster of half-timbered shops: a village plucked out of Hampshire or Wiltshire and rolled out like dough over the great plains. This former cow town, chicken town, egg town hunched its several shoulders together and kept one eye out on the limitless prairie to the west, the other on the merging lines of train track that pointed without a curve or a wiggle to Carl Sandburg's Chicago. The point was to steer clear of the creeks, to huddle in close, to count on the safety and comfort of the trains. For the first hundred years few of the streets, paved or unpaved, strayed for as much as a mile from the station.

And there were, even when we arrived, chicken coops

in town. Perhaps every third house (except in the new martian "developments") had a highly individualized network of outbuildings: coops, pens, barns, dilapidated and vine-strangled arbors of lattice. Chickens clucked and scratched around the coops. In one unearthly elm-shaded and cool yard near us a resident who never showed his face kept two powerful rams chained to a ring set in concrete. Guardian rams. What was it they guarded in the sumac grove? We were warned not to probe. It was explained to me that a boy's leg caught in one of the ram's chains would be severed like a twig.

It was back behind the houses, through their hedges, working stealthily through the ancient cities of these out-buildings that one heard and felt the ache. When the wind whipped itself up into a hard flap in mid-July, turning the wrens and jays out of the trees, off the telephone wires, turning your head with it, you felt it asking something of you, speaking of something important from before the town's time.

Maybe it was not what the town was saying; perhaps it was what the prairie was saying underneath the town. It seemed to speak, or to cry, from everywhere. The message, spoken in waves of wind and in the silences between, seemed to say, "Something important has happened. It is not over." I have been back recently, as a grown man in a grown man's clothes, and the cries can still be heard. This was at first hard even for me to believe. Back to town for a school reunion after an absence of twenty years, I trod the remembered streets for miles one solitary Friday. There was indescrib-able sweetness and the old aching, in spite of the fact that all of the chicken coops had disappeared—they were certainly illegal. Rams guarded no sumac-encircled groves. Groves had given way to lawns. The town had paved the scruffy green verge along the train trestle where in thickets bums used to pass the night like corpses swaddled in rags. The half-timbered shops of the old village were crowded out of prominence by larger, blocklike and weirdly insubstantial buildings of glass, aluminum, and plastics textured to look like stone. The old pie-shaped bank was done over in corrugated metal of gray-green, so that it looked like some monstrous toy ship beached on the teeming pavement. Traffic does teem there now. Traffic may be the town's present theme. The train station is gone, razed perhaps with the sentinel elms.

But, as I said, the cries persist. They persist behind the garages of the older houses, in those hard-to-tend ells between wall and fence where skunk cabbage asserts itself like a right, where garter snakes regenerate themselves and leave their skins. Between the walkways of the older public playground and the hedges of the frame houses abutting it, I heard it—even saw it—distinctly. Beneath and between the base stalks of each bush were inviting, dirt-lined "entrances" into darkness and tangle, a hint only of green, not of houses, beyond, entrances big enough for a midsize dog or a smallish boy. Slightly wet, quivering and straining with each gust, the bushes beckoned in the old way.

The presence in the prairie did not depend on the prairie. It does not now and it did not, really, when I was a boy and the prairie stretched westward from the rim of the town like a personality.

The prairie—we called it The Fields—was an early confirmation of divinity-on-earth.

> Backing on the convent
> Was a prairie full of pale green hay,
> Green in April, otherwise
> Tufted up in wheat-bleached whirls
> Like twisted tops of brooms
> Brushed over the flat expanse

Skirting farms with weathered barns
Highway streaked, cracked by creeks,
Mouse tickled and pheasant scratched
For a thousand prairie miles
Beyond the skyline's hazy edge.

Hiking, crawling, bellying under and over the fields of high grass, the creek banks, the marshy thickets of sumac and scrub, I understood the primitive impulse to *map out* turf. The retreading of familiar steps, especially in a wilderness, serves to imprint that turf in the brain. External geography is not real until it becomes internal geography. I charted an intricate expanse that covered miles of fields beyond the town's edge, knew every thicket, every tractor path, the depth and feel of each bend in the creek, knew which of the slender scrub trees would support a climber's weight and which tangle of bush and branch was waste and which was likely to give up a crazed rabbit.

And there were those breathtaking stands of poplars (planted in such straight lines to demarcate property?) against deep blue late afternoon skies—or, sometimes, against orange-pink sunset, which, when it happens, is pure holiness. What are those poplars about? They seem to me now to be about France, about forgotten, quiet times when rural people went about their business, worlds away from Caesar or Charlemagne or Napoleon. A chapter in the *Ancient Rome* book my students read is called "The Long Twilight." It is a rich and full account of how in the provincial parts of the politically hopeless Empire—Britain south of the Wall, Gaul west of the Rhine, and in all the rolling, habitable places south of the Danube—life went on, even prosperously, even sweetly. Along the East Anglian fens, across the dusk-lit fields of Brittany, provincial souls surely ached with the fullness of the long twilight: gazing at and beyond stands of poplars on the horizon.

41

The fields beyond the edge of town were glutted with animals—not deer, which the farmers had cajoled and herded into forest preserves regulated by the state of Illinois. But the animals that are part of the texture of the prairie itself are indomitable: buckwheat-colored rabbits, squirrels, chucks, muskrats, possum, skunk, shaggy rats, river rats, chipmunks, field mice, black snakes, garter snakes, and corn snakes. Because our fields were not farmed or cut, they would, on hot, dry, July mornings, shiver and hiss with snakes starting and twisting away from our footsteps: a glimpse only of their khaki and stripes through the bleached swirls of grass. Khaki and stripes—they all wore the same clothes: chipmunk, garter, toad, grasshopper, badger, beaver, even the forgotten fawn.

At his—at my—core the boy is, like Narcissus at his pool, trying to get back to something, trying to join it, merge with it. Spring thaws the impulse; July excites it to boiling. Boy's eye meets bird's eye with an inarticulate thrill, moves to it, would hold it in his hands if he could. He would—and this is true—kill it.

Killing is a little-investigated expression of the impulse to have. Thoreau knew about it. He said he would never trust a pacifist who had not evolved through his urge to hunt. Every boy at his core knows the urge. I am not sure that girls know it.

Killing is an extension of sweet desire, of a primal love—which sounds wretched, perverse. Moreover, it *is* wretched and perverse, the impulse spoiled the instant it becomes understood: when it becomes a conscious intention. Only in deep alienation, in the most depressed illnesses and in the cheapest "art" is the *self-conscious* killing of the beloved celebrated as profound. But for boys, for a spell in their time, the desire for animals and the desire to kill them are fused. So sweet and so deeply pulsing is the fusion that

42

civilized restraints on its expression (although very important for civilization) do not diminish it in the least. The drive overpowers restraint, overpowers gentler affections. It spills over its bearer, and it spills over the living objects of desire. It can so overcome the killer than even the means of killing—the dagger, the bow, the arrow, the rifle—become charged with it. Men even now, arrested here, make idols of their weapons. They oil stocks. They sift bullets through their fingers like coins. They feel, and even dully express, that the sweetness, the power is somehow *in the gun*. Potential slaughter lies this way, and it has always lain that way.

The boy's eye instantly closes the distance between self and the bird on the wire. The rabbit hounded out of bramble and zigzagging wildly out of reach is frozen in the boy's mind's eye. There is a furry fold between the shoulder and the neck, a soft vulnerability, a target.

Imaginary hunts preoccupy the boy at rest. Simulated hunts fill his play. Halting, hopeless, half-understood hunts direct his wandering through prairie and thicket. There may be a gun, toy or not. There may be a longing for a gun.

> I dreamed of rifles
> On the wall, ownable, heft in my hands,
> The shoulder fit of the oiled stock,
> An eye down the dull blue barrel.
>
> Cocking one with a clink I could feel it
> Tense inside, over-ready.
> Finger joint cool on the trigger's curve,
> Fondling, refitting itself,
> A certain tickle of control;
> The firm pull would be final.
>
> Once there was a rifle, a toy.
> A blue tin facsimile.
> But I could cock it,

Set a spring and shoot
Hard corks across the living room
Or at the line of plastic crows
Clipped upon a wire rack.
Cork-struck, they dropped
And clicked like plastic on the hardwood,
A slight recognition
In each tinny kill.

So few guns would shoot.
Lightweight pistols lined with flimsy springs
Launched plunger-headed plastic darts
Puckering onto a pane of glass.
Maybe. Maybe at first.
Then the flash and bone of western guns,
Rhinestone-holstered handfuls—

One wide morning in a summer field,
I draw suddenly on something in the tree line
And shoot: a cap cracks the clearness.
The sweet char of its powder
Reminds me of something,

And I pass between the sun and form
Of an old mythic bird,
Dead again in the grass.
Again its stillness startles—

Bone-beaked, feather edges fine as snakeskin:
Prey. I am pre-Indian
Standing over pre-Eagle.
Before the bison or the bow
I was sinew and spear,
A sense of skull, of flank, of tender throat,
The cat's night eye,
A pounce.

Before the rifle (smuggled against permission into the
garage) there was a year of the bow and arrow. *Father—*

44

what a lapse! The bow was as tall as I was, and I could string it only with arm-trembling exertions. The four blue-feathered, silver-tipped arrows I quickly lost, shot past all finding in the fields, and replacements were purchased at the hardware store in town. *Merchants—where did you imagine those arrows would fly?* Into straw-backed targets? Into cardboard boxes? No, they were fired dreamily up into the undersides of eagles, dead into the swollen guts of bears. Rabbits, foxes, and weasles were stuck clear through, dead instantly, as if frozen by the arrow shafts.

There were never enough arrows. Two or three were bounty. A shot into the Fields, if it was a shot of any distance, was almost certainly a lost arrow. Yet every afternoon of a late, cold, darkening autumn a friend and I, equally entranced by the lure of the kill, padded over the frosty tufts of prairie grass, our toes, fingertips, noses raw with the cold. The lower the sun behind the poplars and behind the ravaged stalks of corn, the creamier the grassy way before us. In that light the swirls of spent grasses were transformed from tans to peach to rose. Only a few times did I see the full cycle into soft grays and blues as night fell. (These outings entailed, besides the loss of supper, angry reprisals and promised confinements.)

What were we expecting with our numbing fingers wrapped around the varnished curve of our bows, our two or three mangy arrows rattling over our backs in their makeshift quivers? We expected deer. We expected a majestic buck. He would step unexcitedly out of a thicket and pause before us, the hoof of one foreleg raised slightly above the turf. He would see us but look beyond us. Then our arrows would pierce him, would make him ours. We could know this passionately, relegating the knowledge of forest preserves to the insubstantial realm of common sense and recent history.

There is a margin of time at dusk on a prairie—the hour when tans blur into rose—when a deer, when even a lion, could emerge before a boy. But in spite of this knowledge we were frightened almost senseless when, in the course of stalking noisily over some spent corn rows, not one, not two, but three pheasants, pheasants rampant, roared up out of the stubble right in front of us. I knew as I drew back my arrow (far too late) that I was no match for the pheasants' magnificence. I might just as well have thrown my arrows at them or made a face. Once projected up into the darkening blue, the pheasants became pure silhouette and glided off in a great arc. Far behind them, far too low, our arrows rose, wobbled, and fell back to earth, lost in a thick stand of scrub. Waves of feeling—reverence and loss—silenced us. We made a show of looking for our lost arrows, but it was rapidly darkening, and it was very cold. My friend said he had to go home; we were both inexcusably late.

I would not go. I was near tears, and I could not explain it. I was *there*, I had arrived, I was standing plumb in the middle of rosy, mythic light I had longed for. Three magnificent fowl, shimmering like honey, in green, in deep red, had risen like flags to confirm it, and I had failed even to touch it. Another great bird arose. Before I reached for my last arrow, I knew how futile my "shot" would be; the very realization weakened my arms and my trembling fingers. Once again my arrow arched feebly below the trajectory of the pheasant. *If I could not touch these things,* I cried out loud, *why was I there?*

That night I could not sleep for the obsessive reconstruction of the first pheasants' rising. Even in imagination, I could not hold the bow still, could not hold the birds still against the stained glass sky and propel my loving shot through the bones of their breasts. I had been there, but I was just a boy with a boy's bow and two cheap arrows.

I hardened against that hurt. Not far from our house

there was a houseful of brothers who had guns, big boys, who shot to kill. Their talk was all of killing, that and the other secrets. There was something hard, something dead about their company. Even their laughter was deadening—it was more like shouting than laughing. They stole from stores. They kept a large, greasy envelope of obscene photographs in which the naked men and women thrust their exposed parts defiantly toward each other or in the direction of the viewer. They were angry pictures. The naked men and women had the same eyes as the brothers who owned the photographs. They all seemed to have a hunch about me. Would I like to drive their old man's car? (I was nine.) Would I dare fire a .38 caliber pistol up into a streetlight?

One bitingly cold November afternoon I followed their hunched shoulders into the Fields. Wedged carelessly under their arms were rifles, gas compression pellet guns, and .22s. I wanted guns like that, I dreamed of guns like that, and the big boys knew it. The prairie was dead, but a rabbit might be scared up, a pheasant might rise up into the soot and steel sky.

There was nothing. Nose and chin, lips and jaw became as numb as a drunk's. Finger grew stiff, the rim of each ear burned with the cold. Then somebody spotted a few gray birds—wrens—perched on the prickly twig-fingers of a stand of trees along the creek. They were so remote and so insubstantial that they might have been bits of dead leaf. One of the dead-eyed boys took aim with his pellet rifle and fired a muffled pop into the tree line. Even to his surprise, one of the leaf-bit-birds dropped off its branch and zigzagged sickeningly downward into the grass.

We ran to it. Incredibly tiny, batlike, its legs drove its injured torso around in a circle. There was a dark red hole at the base of the bird's neck, in which a glimpse of metal pellet could be seen. The gray bird seemed to be skewered to the earth by the pellet in its neck. Its bright black eye saw nothing. The bald little legs would grow still, then start spasmodically, driving the damaged torso around the hub of its pain. That tiny bird charged the whole prairie—perhaps the whole cosmos—with terror and pain.

"Your turn," a dead-eyes said to me. "Kill it." He pumped the rifle and handed it to me. He had never let me fire it before.

"Kill it, and it's your bird."

He guided the barrel of the rifle so it rested on the bird's pulsing head.

"Kill it."

I looked off into the tree line and squeezed the trigger.

"Bye, bird." Their laughter hung in the cold like pain. One of them made a show of crushing the spent little carcass underfoot, and they moved on, toward home. They let me carry the rifle. All the tractor path home, then into the night, then into other nights, still into this night, I am pulsing with the wounded bird, my eyes following the unnatural circuitry of its pain, its neurons, its vessels, its spine, its connectedness to air and tree and prairie smashed and severed by a small shard of lead. I am still on the brink of firing the shot I fired then.

Soon after the shooting, the world stopped presenting itself to me as being continually alive: a living fabric of earth and grass, at times crawling with, at times concealing, an amplitude of animals. The *continuous* impression stopped, but there would be—and still are—powerful reminders. It can be a reminder frozen in a painting, as in Breughel's *Hunters in the Snow*. People of Illinois know that weather and that light, I know; I learned the numb-footed, numb-lipped return from the hunt over dead, snow-patched turf. I know the green in the gray of winter skies, how the cold penetrates every layer, how it can freeze and emphasize

48

distances yet to walk. No one would waste a word in that weather, walking that ground.

But one midsummer afternoon in the north of Michigan it all came back to me. My family had taken a vacation cottage on a clear, cold lake. I had reached an age, twelve, where Michigan no longer *meant* the tug of pike far beneath the glassy surface of gold-brown water. The sharp-sweet pine, the tang of which, mixed with earth, damp, and cooking, rose up and tantalized me even inside the cabin. It was in the sheets, in the sofa cushions, in the sink drains. It would emanate from the walls and from the wide planks of the floor.

Other things had come up, unsettlingly, to command my attention: less substantial but more insistent. There were, foremost, the inexhaustible rituals of sport. Each sport—baseball, golf, tennis—held out its own elaborate conventions, its attractive (but always subtly changing) nuances, and its gallery of local, national, and mythic heroes. Not to mention the equipment. Sculptures in oiled leather, miraculously polished wooden shafts and frames, gleaming clubheads, somehow both bulbously heavy and sharp-edged, bottle-handled bats, creamy new baseballs, the culs-de-sac of the cowhide's red stitches blurring into my concentration just before my air-creasing swing. Every summer morning opened into the swirl and drill and news of sports, but the North Woods was not the place for it; the North Woods suspended the noise.

One still and steamy afternoon there, left alone while the rest of the family fished, I struck out aimlessly on a footpath into the woods. Without looking, eyes on the path, I passed beyond the ring of cottages, through the thick, low pines, even through gradations of terrain hardly noticed onto more open, airier ground. The trees were silver birches, and they flickered their higher leaves like bright coins in the

49

breezes. There was movement now. The ground fell away on one side of the path, dropping into the bed of a fast and forceful stream. The stream pushed itself noisily over and around rocks and fallen timber. In the shallows, dappled tan and white, the stream glossed over smooth stones, then darkened into deeper pools of root beer brown.

Mindlessly hurried along by the stream, I happened onto a wide, sandy flat, where the current splayed out to the width of a little river. Ahead of me the birches and scrub circled around and closed the path, but by fording the sandy shallows, I could cross the stream and proceed into what looked like range after range of pale sand dunes, creamy-looking in the late afternoon night.

There, midstream, the clear water rippling over the soles of my shoes, something underneath the surface caught my eye. The floor of the stream bed, seemingly composed of sand and stones, began to move beneath the water like a slow kaleidoscope of earth tones. There was a quick intimation of "other laws" taking hold. I did not resist. I watched with a thrill as a cluster of mottled rocks before me became sizable crayfish which, perhaps disturbed by my step, scuttled over the sand away from me. Then, as if sent to verify my trespass and to file a report, the lacquered snouts of four or five brown trout appeared about an invisible circumference perhaps a yard from where I stood. They hovered there in tense precision like a line of bombers. Their iridescent browns, honey, and spangles picked up perfectly the camouflage of the crayfish, of the afternoon light over the rippled surface, and the dappled bottom cover. Next, as if to reveal to the adjusted eye even more elemental components of stream, dark minnows began shooting like needles through the composition, drawn forward in delicate parallels, then veering sharply away, as if filings before an unseen magnet.

Anything seemed possible in that enchanged light, provided I did not take a step. How long did I stay? A few seconds? An hour and a half? However long, it was rosy twilight, the water gone to dark glass, by the time I sloshed onto the dune side of the stream. I was half-willing to proceed over the dunes to an unseen Lake Superior, even, if I could have expressed it, to the Nile or to Arcady. But I took only a step or two, for out of the scrub along the stream's edge appeared a lovely doe and her fawn, mute and regal. Again the intimation: *other laws*.

What happened next would surely have been surprising at another time. But in this particular procession of events in which stones had become crustaceans, leaves mantises, the blacker scars on the birches wizened bats, it seemed inevitable that other deer, what must have been a herd of deer, would materialize out of the scrub and take their stately places at the stream's edge. Even in zoos or when otherwise domesticated, deer call one fleetingly back to an earlier time. Each wants to say something, some gentle warning. Like cats, both genders are profoundly feminine. Deer have been hurt so much and for so long that they can only take flight or implore. There were about forty of them that evening. They were spaced along the curve of the stream. Each would drink silently, then draw back upright and still, alert to twilight signals available only to a deer.

There I stood in the middle of it: a secret open to me— and perhaps opening still. Would wolves come down to drink? Panthers? I could spoil it with a shout, with a stomp of my foot, with a splash. Who would believe it? Who would even share it with me? I walked home.

I wanted to explain it but got no further than describing the path. I did not know how to begin to tell the truth about it. The facts, the words I knew did not say enough: I saw a lot

51

of crayfish and fish and deer. Not even a photograph would contain what I saw. I said I took a hike and that it was really great.

I deliberated hard about asking my family to return with me to the enchanted spot. Even now I am not sure whether the thing I dreaded most was that when we reached the ford, there would be nothing to see—or that they *would* see what I had seen, and the very fact of so much publicity would disenchant the experience forever. As it happened I did not take anybody to the spot, but I returned a few days later, alone.

I took off on this second solitary hike just after bright noon and wondered whether this would alter everything. The walk seemed longer. The path was muggy and buggy, but the gusts that brushed through the birches and the pines stirred up enough sense of deep solitude that another powerful transformation seemed at least possible. Would it be the same? Did I really want it to be the same?

Just at the point where the path terminated and, around a bend of scrub, the stream splayed out into the sandy flat, I stopped. Had it ever really happened? Had I dreamed all that life? The answer came crackling noisily from my left. A large doe shouldered her way out of the thick scrub and stopped still about ten yards ahead of me on the path. With the calm of a cow, she swung her head in my direction and appeared to consider me thoughtfully. Satisfied of something, she turned away and stepped unhurried around the bend to the rushing water. Satisfied myself, I ran home.

God
and Saints

How does the idea of God come into one's life? The question, put that way, is a little misleading. God is certainly imminent in anybody's life—and therefore does not "enter." What comes in, I believe at a point in late infancy or early childhood, is a name for it, along with some kind of first conceptual framework with which to make sense of one's most vivid experiences of God.

The words, including the right words, seep in from the outset. There is God, a kind of man-force, presiding over creation like a father-king. There is the God of holidays, of anthems, graces, and prayers—this is a safer, civic God. But *connecting* the God-name to the God-experience is a complex and subtle process, one that may, literally, go every which way.

Religious instruction sometimes deadens or obscures the understanding of divinity. Put very simply, from earliest consciousness one has very powerful experiences of being connected to creation. Then, somewhat later in the development of consciousness, "religious" ideas are introduced.

My own religious ideas did not connect to my most vivid personal experiences until well after my schooling had commenced. I know this to be the case because my earliest school memories are shot through with a kind of natural pantheism. It was without question a world of wonders, but only later, and through inspired help, would I see a design in it.

By the time I was enrolled in kindergarten, I was aware of having reached a very secure level of citizenship. I belonged in school. The order of that earliest classroom seemed to have—and arguably did have—centuries of force behind it. School and township and state were one. Like so many boys before and since, I would not be able to understand school, nor to love it properly, until I could exercise some control over it. Why don't schoolteachers understand this better? My earliest gesture of affection toward my schooling was truancy. Even in the heaven of my kindergarten, I played "hard to get."

The floor was brown linoleum. The air was sweet with wax and paste: the usual smells of school. And all of us so small in corduroy, our rubber boots lined up like ducks, obedient beneath the coatrack. Outside, above the mammoth windows April sun, half-hidden, shone, spraying sometimes, nonetheless, yellow warmth like arms around our gladdened shoulders.

Three of us were very good at bolting boards together for a castle; you could even crawl inside it in the created dark and whisper of the newness. There was Gerald, though, his trousers hiked up chokingly, who lived to knock things down.

He slapped the girls across their faces. On the walk back home, a stone from him could crease your head to bloody stitches. Once it did. We knew, much more than now, of evil: staring, unpredictable as Gerald's watchful eyes.

Gwendolyn would never talk. School had shocked her out of speech, but otherwise she functioned normally, puttering with puzzle parts, dreaming they were pots and pans. She smiled often but never spoke; to us this was her dignity.

We were, I think, a pleasant herd, a few rough edges, bumpy, somewhat slow at forming lines, fidgety when read to and variously tone deaf; but always there on time, the same size, the same hats. There were few criers, little scuffling. We used the toilet quietly, thoughtfully regarding familiar knees below the door. We buckled down for smiles, pats, and compliments, decently disposed to weigh the issues put before us: justice or fruit juice served in paper cups, half filled and never quite enough. In timeless clatter mornings passed.

At ten o'clock the rugs were spread like patches across the floor. The time for naps the state prescribed, like trains stopped steaming in the village, like china set for Sunday noon, like the drop of darkness stopping play, time was marked inevitably. It was all the same to us. The oily shades were pulled down dark. Some of us lay solemnly, hearing just the clock cranking minutes. No one slept. The ritual was restful, reminding us of isolation, firm as cold linoleum beneath our shaggy rugs.

Inclined to grope at customs for their edges, I slithered on my rug beneath Miss Vanderkellan's desk. Dark there. Upside down, I mustn't breathe. The comfortable cut of two black flats spoke of her endearingly. Not to mention shiny stockings sheer along her sculptured calves.

Aesthetics were enough for just a minute in a nap of time—especially faced, as I was with a pair of shoes, coy and intimate as someone known nearly well enough to kiss. Lightly as I could, I scratched a toe and watched as it withdrew, mindless of the cause. A pause. I scratched again, determinedly. On hands and knees, her face peered at me, enormously.

"Just what are you doing, please?" she spoke in nap-regarding tones. The situation, it seemed to me, was plain beyond explaining. "Nothing" seemed appropriate. "Resting," for clarity. "I see," she said. "Come out of there, we need to have a talk." She sat me on a stool beside her in the darkened room, so private, sitting high above the nappers knotted naturally as patchwork.

"You know, I'm sure you know," she said, "we stay in school till twelve o'clock." (My answer was to keep from blinking.) "At recess you've been running off. Haven't we been through this once before? Would you like it if I never let you out at all?" (If only I could keep from blinking.) "For that might be what I should do in order to keep track of you. What would it be like if *I* ran off one morning?" I considered: "No juice" is what first came to mind. "That's right, no juice, no school. You would all be sent back home. Home—is that where you run off to when I turn my back?"

No, not really home; more the solitude along the way, immersed in green and April wind, last fall the apples falling green and bitter by the Parkers' porch. The round, compelling bush in the park, still budding, where once a bird from somewhere else, no bigger than an acorn and colored like a book of gems, streamed its emerald tail and hummed its fanning wings in fright. Painlessly, I pushed my fingers through the tearing brambles to its singing center; signals from another world, like vernal dreams of naked pasts, must be grabbed and held if parks and dreams would meet in meaning. Somehow the tiny thing ascended, its frantic humming mirrored in my anxious heart. Free, it moved away

56

from me, whirring upright, backing farther, farther off: a warning angel whisked away by wind. My hand was stinging hotly in the April cold. Home? No. I don't know really where I go.

"Well, one thing must be understood, young man," her hands upon my shoulders, firmly as her words were soft. "You must not disappear again. You know where you belong. There are lots of things here we can do, lots to build, and lots of friends. The streets are full of cars. Your mother worries. I do, too. So promise me you understand and won't go running off again." I promised her I understood, since it was true. I did.

At a word the rugs were shifted to a circle for a story: a little circus bear was on a train ride through the forest, but the tracks cracked, the cars broke, and out he rode on a one-wheeled bike, the goofiest thing in the woods. In a bright red coat his figure eights made all the big bears laugh. (They meant to give him trouble, though.) But backward and forward he pedaled and zipped, no hands, one foot, and a winsome grin, and the big bears' laughs got happy. So they all made friends, and a little she-bear with little blue shoes, hopped on his shoulders, and they pedaled off to loving, and the big bears followed, two by two.

The story topped the morning like a pointed peak; now to slide its sunny side in play outside the schoolroom. Hats were snapped beneath our chins. Boots burped and squeaked beneath our clumsy, stooping steps. Scarf-swaddled, we formed a crowd, cut to a jumpy double file by Miss Vanderkellan's hand. I was paired with Gwendolyn, a quiet sort of privilege. Approved, we marched outdoors.

April crisp and blowy as the sky was blue in parts. A few false starts, then bedlam and a scramble for the green. The swarm revolved, and I unseen, breathed deep and clear, calculating the speed required to vanish past the boundary hedge. Then sudden on my rubber soles, I glided through the bicycles, across the street, across the park, beyond the lilac sentries to the promise of surprise.

Perhaps the most instructive surprise occurred in the summer of my sixth year when I was nearly drowned in a Wisconsin lake. A nonswimmer, but increasingly sure of myself around the water's edge, I got hold of an inner tube someone had temporarily discarded on the beach, draped myself into it supine, and began paddling myself, with surprising effect, away from shore. It was a bakingly hot August afternoon in which beach babble mixed with the muted hum of outboard motors. Silently and very high overhead a jet left a chalky vector against the blue. Feeling utterly the master of my acquired craft and also a little sleepy, I could not have been more unprepared for the shock to come.

I thought I had paddled beyond the range of the swimmers, but I was mistaken, because one glistening otter of a boy, perhaps fifteen, had silently made his way out to me underwater and, in a powerful upward surge, surfaced through the opening of my inner tube and upended me into the lake. As I went under, eerily aware of exactly what had happened, I was perfectly resigned to death. The water was perhaps eight to ten feet deep; I was four feet tall and was, as I have said, not yet a swimmer. As I sank, time expanded marvelously. I do not think I panicked, even to the extent of flailing my arms—which, undoubtedly, would have helped to raise me to the surface. Rather, I descended, feet first, eyes open, through fine gradations of tans and browns. I was dropping darkeningly out of the world, out of life. I remember no unpleasant physical sensation, such as running short of breath, only a progression from the bright surface of the lake, up over the edge of the back rubber inner tube, the glistening torso of my assailant, noise, then down into the muted, increasingly private murkiness.

Without reflection I began saying the Lord's Prayer. I do not think I said it in desperation, certainly not in hope, because I had none. I was, if memory serves, preparing a way for the next world, the existence of which, at that moment, I was certain, although I cannot remember any prior contemplation of life after death. Nor do I remember when or the circumstances under which I learned the Lord's Prayer. I must have heard it (although our family's churchgoing history at that time was spotty), but it was not a nightly prayer. By the time I had mentally prepared the phrases, "Thy kingdom come, thy will be done," I felt ready. This was an important event, this descent, but it was not "wrong"; this was, I was sure, the way experience was supposed to unfold. I felt from that instant very much a passenger, now moving mysteriously through a medium of dark water, whereas less than a minute earlier I had been a passenger—different time frame, less fully awake—through a medium of bright, breathable air.

Then I was rescued. The boy who had upended me had been more interested in the elegance of the feat than in winning the inner tube or in drowning a skinny little boy. Hoisted up to the surface by the armpits, I was reinserted into the inner tube by my cheerful assailant and savior. Full now of practicality, I thrashed and kicked my way into the safe sandy-bottomed shallows where, dully, I passed the rest of the afternoon.

Throughout my boyhood and afterward I have periodically relived that "accident" in an attempt to explain it. Where had the prayer come from? From whence the *efficacy* (the great calm, not the rescue) of the prayer? Perhaps in consequence of the event's having aroused such engaging

59

questions, it was more than coincidence that in the years immediately following I would become profoundly involved with two boys, each of whom talked, in his idiosyncratic way, to God daily. I believe both of them are great saints. Neither would have seen anything other than God's hand in my submersion and rescue.

It is a great thing and a refreshing thing to meet someone for whom God is real. Clergymen—including a few I have met who hold theological distinction—do not always, or even usually, convey the impression that God is real. But Kevin Conley, an eccentric neighbor during my first years of schooling, wrestled with God as intensely as Jacob did and inadvertently initiated me into great mysteries.

Kevin Conley was, before all other allegiances, a Roman Catholic. And, rather in the manner of Tom Sawyer whitewashing his fence, he made a non-Catholic like me long for the terrors and the intricate rituals of his faith. He was a big-boned, big-toothed blond boy three years older than I. He had not originally intended to befriend me. In fact we met when he came over to our newly built suburban house to throw stones at my sister and me. Even before our arrival he and his sisters—Constance, Grace, and Gloria—loathed and cursed our coming. Our house, he told me later, was built over a pleasant forest of sumac where the Conleys had once happily played. Kevin Conley liked me because I listened with fascination to everything he said and did his bidding like a disciple, but he never entirely gave up his impulse to punish me.

What he said was fascinating. He was driven by forces that had not yet come to bear on my life: consuming fear, esthetic ecstasy, unto-death loyalty, prayerful reverence. An early memory of Kevin is of his standing in deep reverie one Sunday morning before a great burst of lilacs. His hair was wetted heavily down on his head, and he was unnaturally dressed up in a white shirt and a necktie. But the wonderful thing about his appearance that morning was that the orbit around one eye was garishly discolored to violet, purple, and black. I had never before seen a black eye, and I have not seen one since as spectacular as Kevin's. Even now, the sight of a lilac tree in bloom brings to mind that marbled bruise.

Kevin himself was elated by his wound and by the chain of events that had produced it. His mother had hit him. In the hectic process of preparing her noisy family for mass, she had corrected and scolded several of her children including, finally, Kevin. He had answered her back, had been warned, answered the warning insolently, and had been smacked, hard, alongside his eye. As is so often the case, her own violence, underscored by wild cries of pain from Kevin, unraveled Mrs. Conley. She tried to apologize and to console, but Kevin ran off. By the time the family had assembled to get into the car for mass, the eye had already assumed a startling, raccoonlike prominence. This was too much for Mrs. Conley, a highly strung woman in any event, and she dissolved in tears. This moved Kevin deeply. Feelings of profound psychological triumph mingled with deep sympathy for his mother. As he told me about it, he caressed a crisp new dollar bill his mother had given him in compensation. "She is going to bring it up in confession," Kevin explained. He added that he had already forgiven her to God during mass and had forgiven her "out loud" in the car on the way home.

I wanted to know about confession, and he told me. What followed was the most satisfying conversation I believe I have ever had. First came an engrossing account of mortal and venial sins, upon which my mind would turn agitatedly throughout my childhood. The idea of such sins, the venial especially, seemed to me to be so fundamentally right—and at the same time so fresh and so unexpected. You were never, Kevin Conley told me, to call another person a "fool." You were not to throw away money, not even a penny. A Catholic must never enter a non-Catholic church or take part in any non-Catholic worship. As single-mindedly gluttonous as the next child, I was fascinated by the idea of gluttony— that the phenomenon I knew so well had a name. I was awed that holy men—Catholics—had been thinking about it for centuries. The very word—"gluttony"—took hold of me. There seemed even to be a kind of metaphysical meat, at once irresistible and disgusting, called "glutton," that represented all other foods. (Years later when I read Joyce's *Ulysses,* it occurred to me that the combination of awfulness and savoriness of the kidney eaten by Bloom was the very essence of "glutton.")

It began to break my heart that I was by virtue of my parents' decision to be Presbyterian to be excluded from so much Catholic richness. I grew wild in my longing for all the things from which, as a non-Catholic, I would be forever excluded. Mass itself—a prayerful process which in my imagination took place under dark nets—confession, cate-chism, limbo (a stratum of dimly lit, half-dead bodies), winged angels and saints, altar boys, rosaries, and all the mortal and venial sins belonged to the lively, ancient world of the Catholics. The thought that Kevin could not intention-ally enter the Presbyterian church, our church, obsessed me. Over the course of our friendship I tried to lure him inside many times, never with success. Big and learned and confi-dent as he was, the idea of spiritual adverturism was repug-nant to him because, he believed, he was strict in every observance he understood. Thus he would never knowingly eat meat on a Friday, with the understanding that Friday terminated precisely at midnight, as registered by his kitchen clock. More than once when I slept over at his house for the night, I waited up with him in the bright kitchen as he stood like a soldier beside a plate of sliced bologna and white bread.

Nor was his faith confined to ritual. He would never ride his bike past the carcass of a wren or robin on the street without dismounting, bowing his head, and uttering a silent prayer for its soul. He was not sure if birds rose into the heaven of human beings, but he knew that they rose at least into a heaven of their own. The idea of a heaven exclusively for animals appealed to me very much; I thought of it as a warmer, fairer heaven. I was impressed that Kevin Conley's concern for the souls of departed animals extended beyond the familiar and the cute: birds, squirrels, cats, etc. Bloated earthworms, too, nakedly exposed on the wet pavement after a rain, received his benedictions. The rightness of these blessings struck something deep within me. Today, thirty years later, I cannot pass a mutilated animal carcass on the berm of the highway without commending its soul to God.

Kevin saw the souls of the human dead as ghostly apparitions. He reported several sightings to me in the course of our friendship. The first I can remember hearing about was the visible ascension up through the roof of his house of an uncle of Kevin's called Daddy Mac. *Immediately after the death* of a Catholic, Kevin explained, the soul can be seen hovering weightless above the body. "It's there for about fifteen minutes." This rang true. When I looked out over the roofline of the Conley's house, it was easy to picture the vaporous form of Kevin's Daddy Mac rising into the sky like a balloon.

Spiritually alive as he was, Kevin was always a faintly disturbing presence in my company. He carried with him a sense of being hunted—a condition frequently based in actual circumstances. An outspoken, daring boy, he seemed always to pose an affront, a challenge to anybody older than he was. Something about the way he asserted himself, the way he arrived on the scene, the flourish with which he would dismount his bicycle, seemed to say: "Take me and what I have to say as authoritative—or annihilate me." Many people of the town—older boys and, for some reason, many fathers, including his own—would like to have annihilated Kevin Conley.

He caused conventional trouble, in which I was whenever possible, a rapt accomplice, but he always did it within the imaginative context of an important cause or an elaborate game. Thus when we torched the bushes of a vacant lot on our block, seriously threatening the immolation of many houses, his object was not destruction or mayhem, it was to provide the opportunity for spectacular fire fighting.

Especially memorable was his campaign, in which I am ashamed to say I participated energetically, to prevent the completion of a Christian Science church under construction next door to his house. He was very bitter about the church. For one thing, yet another numinous, thicket-rich meadow had been eliminated from his range of play. For another, in Kevin's opinion, the Christian Scientists were anathema to Catholicism. The explanation, something about not believing in doctors, was lost on me, but I found his hostility infectious. It was easy to be mad at this great ugly edifice of new red brick thrusting itself out of the grove where we had burrowed and climbed, lit forbidden fires.

Kevin felt he could demoralize the builders of the Christian Science church if he broke enough of its windows. He had broken one by accident overthrowing a ball in his yard one evening—and was inspired by the furor he overheard among the builders the following morning. Kevin was not a conventional vandal. He would have been deeply ashamed of himself if he had done something so devious as to throw rocks through the church windows while under the cover of darkness. He preferred indirection, a way of breaking windows that allowed for a divine hand to come into play.

At about five in the afternoon, when the workers would leave the construction site, Kevin and I would haul our softball bats to a great mound of gravel that had been deposited at the rear of the nearly completed church. We would fill our pockets with stones from the pile, back off to a distance of perhaps fifty yards, and proceed to bat the stones, fungo-style, in the direction of the church. If a window was broken, Kevin persuaded me, that was meant to be. As it turned out, quite a few were fated to be broken before surveillance became so heavy behind the church that the game had to be curtailed.

Kevin's next move in the campaign to destroy the church was characteristically dramatic. The street side of the lot on which the church was being built was lined with a row of tall elms. "We could kill the trees," Kevin said, and they would fall, some of them, on the church and crush it. He determined that we could kill the trees by pounding nails into their trunks. Kevin pinched a bucket of squat, fatheaded roofing nails from the site, and with our fathers' hammers we busied ourselves for the next several late afternoons pounding the inch-long spikes into the lower perimeter of the elms. The magnificence and the subtlety of the plan thrilled me. Kevin liked to talk about how, the day when the first nail-ravaged tree buckled and fell on the church, we would both look up from our play in mock surprise, then nonchalantly go on with our Chinese checkers, or some other docile pursuit.

One afternoon, as supper time approached, a car stopped alongside the tree lawn where we were hammering. The driver, a neighbor named Mr. Preeble, who, Kevin said, hated him, leaned out his car window and challenged us aggressively as to what we were doing. We were just hitting some nails into some trees, Kevin answered back. Mr. Preeble said we had better cut it out immediately, or—the phrase still rings in my ears—he would *call the police.* In fact, he said, he would call the police anyway. Then Mr. Preeble drove off.

Kevin was worried, and I was physically weak with fear. We had been found out—and our crime was, it seemed now, massive in its consequences. We had begun the slaughter of several of the town's greatest trees, trees perhaps already fated to fall on top of a *church,* it occurred to us then, possibly *full of sick people.* We began to try to pull the nails out of the trees with the claw-ends of our hammers. Kevin knew how to do this but was having trouble extracting even one; I could not do it at all. In a few minutes it was clear that there was no undoing what had been so decisively done. The trees were nailed. Kevin suggested that we go home and change our clothes before the police arrived. I have forgotten his exact instructions, but the idea was to be seen looking, so far as I possibly could, like the kind of boy who would not pound nails into trees. "Wear *shorts,*" Kevin ordered, gaining composure as the new plan took shape. "Wear shorts, and wet your hair and comb it *straight back.*"

For days, to my mother's puzzlement, I walked around distractedly in outsize short pants and with my hair pasted back over my head. Like so many other of Kevin's ideas conceived under pressure, the disguises worked. Mr. Preeble, however, would come into our lives again, and that time he would bring the police.

The greatest, most official trouble I have ever gotten into came about in consequence of Kevin's and my shooting Mr. Preeble's son, Carl, in the arms and legs, repeatedly, with our bows and arrows. This was not boyish sadism, although it must sound as if it were. We had bought the bows—disappointingly toylike—at the five-and-dime, but we had replaced the little plunger-headed arrows with green shoots we had broken off from neighborhood hedges. Wobbly in trajectory even within their range of about fifteen yards, these arrows were at least hand-fashioned and "natural." Moreover, their supply was practically unlimited.

One sun-dappled summer morning as we weaved in and out of our neighbors' yards, we came upon the still, inquiring presence of Carl, age six. Although he was a familiar enough figure in our neighborhood, we did not play with him. It was hard to play with him in that he was big and slow in movement, slower still in speech. He was a dark, olive-skinned boy, with full lips, heavy cheeks, and black, liquid eyes. He seemed to have no ideas in his head, not even in response. Because he did not ask us what we were doing, I told him we were hunting. Carl said nothing, but stared at us sullenly, as if we had hurt him.

"Do you want to hunt with us?" I challenged him.

"No," Carl said.

"Do you want us to shoot you with these arrows until you die?" Kevin asked.

"I don't care."

We were sure he cared, or could be made to care. We challenged him, taunted him, warned him to flee. Kevin said he had just shot a cat clear through with one of his forsythia stalk arrows.

"I don't care," Carl said, inert.

"Then I don't care if I shoot your brains out," said Kevin, drawing back an arrow and advancing to a point where its tip was almost touching the boy's ear.

Of course Kevin did not shoot—and would not have shot—Carl Preeble in the head, although he did feel, and so

67

did I, that Carl deserved it. Children and teachers know that it is provocative to be passive and dull, murderously so from the perspective of boys on the hunt.

"Go home," Kevin ordered the boy.

"No. I don't have to."

"What if we shoot you?"

"I don't care."

With that, Kevin backed off a few paces and with diminished force released an arrow in the direction of Carl's profile. It struck him lightly on his bare arm and dropped down onto the grass.

"I don't care," Carl said.

What followed, had it been observed from a distance, must have looked like a protracted and infinitely feeble boys' attempt to re-create the Martyrdom of St. Sebastian. For the rest of the morning until lunchtime, Kevin and I took turns gently launching arrows, interlarded with explanations and irritated warnings, against Carl's stationary bulk. He did not cry, nor did he complain, but in a barely detectable way, perhaps due to the sheer tension created by having stood so long in one spot, he began to register unease. His full, grape-colored lips bunched into a pout.

"You're a son of a bitch," he said to us both, without emotion.

"Are you *mad*?" Kevin asked, excited and amazed.

For a long time Carl said nothing. Then he said, "I don't care."

"How about shooting us for a while?" Kevin asked expansively.

Carl said nothing. Then Kevin almost forcibly instructed Carl as to how to operate the bow. The only difficult part of it, given the crudeness of our arrows, was grooving the bowstring into the blunt, pulpy arrow end. Kevin stood behind Carl, guiding his hand and arms through several trial shots, but Carl had neither the strength nor the dexterity, nor any of the will, to do it himself. When he would draw the bowstring back, the arrow-stick would come away from the bow, wobble madly and then, disengaged from the bowstring, drop down onto the ground.

When it was time to eat, we left Carl standing where we had found him, in the deep green shade of an elderly woman's front lawn. He had not wanted to let go of one of the arrows, so we let him keep it.

The furor began that evening at the dinner hour. We were seated at the table midway through our meal when the enraged shrieking of at least one man and several women drew us powerfully up from the table, out the door, and down the street. It was clear even before the squad cars passed us in a hurry and we saw the cluster of several dozen neighbors bunched on the Conleys' front lawn that the commotion emanated from Kevin's house.

I was excited and the situation was very confused, but a clear memory remains of Mr. Preeble. In his rage, Mr. Preeble's face and neck were the color of raw meat. Dressed in dark trousers and an undershirt with shoulder straps, he was pounding the upper panels of the Conleys' front door with both fists.

"Get out here, Francis Conley, you son of a bitch! Get out here and I'll break your neck." I had never heard Mr. Conley's first name before: Francis.

Inside Mrs. Conley could be heard screaming hysterically, "Will somebody please help us? Will somebody please get him off our *property*? He's going to *kill* us."

The police persuaded Mr. Preeble to step away from the door, and as they guided him down the walk away from the Conleys, Mr. Preeble, still raging, could be heard saying, "Yeah, I'll go home. I *want* to go home. I want you to come home with me, officers. I want you to see what happened to my *son* today. I want you to have a look at what happened to *him*."

As the neighbors broke into uncomprehending, fascinated speculation, my parents sent us home to finish our supper. They would be along later. Vaguely but powerfully, I knew I was in trouble. I knew that enough rage had been loosed in the neighborhood to kill somebody. It could, I believed, kill me. My mind raced back to scan the events of the day. I remembered the slow-motion, irritating morning spent trying to provoke Carl Preeble to make some kind of satisfying gesture. I remembered him, as we left him, standing sullenly in the shade, holding an arrow. Had something happened to him? What had *Mr. Conley* done to him? The idea of Mr. Conley's perhaps unlimited capacity for evil began to terrify me. He had up to that moment, whenever I would play at the Conleys, impressed me as a man of deep, private exasperations. He seemed almost always to be shut into a remote room. When he did appear, it was as if he had passed the limit of human endurance with his family. If he addressed them at all, even to answer a question, it was with a kind of hurt whimper. *"Jesus Christ!"* he would always begin. "Why are you *asking me*?" Kevin and his sisters spoke of him only in dread.

That Mr. Preeble's great rage should be detonated by something in Mr. Conley's own barely suppressed volatility seemed exactly right. The particular *causes* of such detonations are perhaps beside the point: Rage need only look Rage in the face to release itself—one sees this often enough in the conduct of motorists.

When my parents did finally come home, it seemed to me that they had brought a host of people with them: I have the impression of a crowded living room. But they brought only the Preebles. My father called me forth in an alien voice and in a manner that suggested he was not personally

70

related to me. It was a voice for the company, not for me. Stumbling lifeless as a sack of laundry, Carl Preeble was pulled forward by the hand.

"Did you do this to this boy?" My father asked in the foreign voice.

I could not see anything. I could not look at anything.

"Do what?" I asked.

"*This*," somebody said, jerking Carl farther forward, pointing to discolored little circles, raisin-sized bruises or bug bites, dotting his arms and legs.

"We thought he was *sick*, that he had come down with measles or something," said a bewildered Mrs. Preeble. "And we called the doctor. Then Carl told us that Kevin Conley and your boy had been *shooting him with arrows*. That they wanted to *kill* him."

"We didn't try to kill him. We were just—" I did not know what to say. Nobody was talking about the way it had actually happened. "He let us shoot at him. He didn't care."

At this Mr. Preeble said something angrily, perhaps a curse, and my own train of thought was lost in the commotion. It lasted several days. There were a number of conferences, without me, in our living room. There was talk of "it's going to court." I had been to the town courtroom on a school trip. Down the hall from the courtroom was the jail. I was more fascinated than frightened: I had somehow touched, somehow moved the civic apparatus of the greater world. Moved by whatever moved me in play, I had done something that seriously, officially mattered, and it was bad.

But then the event, in the course of so much adult conferring, seemed to veer away from me and Kevin. The overheard talk now turned primarily on the instability and unreasonableness of Mr. Preeble and also, when they were not present, on the instability and the unreasonableness of the Conleys. I was also told repeatedly that Kevin Conley

71

was a "bad influence" on me and that we should not play together. I understood what this meant practically, but it was the first of several instances to follow of parental judgments that failed to connect at all to what I most intimately felt and knew. Kevin Conley was not a "bad influence." But he was an influence. He transformed everything. He was personally in touch with the spirit of things. A hammer, a bird's nest came to life in his hands. He had a quick, rapt appreciation of place, indoors or out. He was alert to the spirits of people and animals, to God himself. He was driven, he was a fighter, and he did some bad things—even he knew that wrecking the Christian Science church was a bad thing. But he was in love with the idea of battle, of great adversaries. The world owed him an enemy, a physical challenge, a risk alive with danger.

In a week the skin on Carl Preeble's arms and legs had cleared up, and so did the cloud of trouble that hovered close around my head. I was allowed to play with Kevin again under restricted conditions until, through lack of conviction, the restrictions were forgotten. What, finally, had we done? Had we hurt or bullied a neighbor boy? I don't think so. I think we encountered a Victim. In his immobility on the shady lawn, in his its-already-happened passivity, his dullness, in the way he clutched our last arrow, in the pox of his little bruises, he was Victim.

The arrow-shooting episode and its tense aftermath served to bring Francis Conley, Kevin's father, into a new prominence. In Norse mythology, as I would learn later, the very cosmos is shot through with malignant forces. In that cosmology the habitable universe is a tree, the leaves of which are being nibbled away by deer, the roots nibbled away by a serpent. Up in the high branches of the tree rests an eagle, and between its lofty perch and the tree's root scampers, for the duration of Time, a squirrel whose sole mission is to convey insults back and forth between the eagle and the serpent. The trunk of the tree is rotten. In such a world, wonderful in its hostile dynamics, Francis Conley assumed an honored place.

Mr. Conley was not a large man, but his face seemed somehow massive. He had an unhealthy, dangerous-looking pallor, the color of his skin, when he was at rest, nearly lavender. His eyes were tiny and bright and were set deeply into his head. His hair swept straight back over his head in a series of sharply creased waves—the kind of hair which, like the hair of former President Richard Nixon, had always made me reflexively uneasy. He was coiled unbearably tight. He seemed to vibrate with inner tension. I could hear it in his reedy voice, which could rise to terrifying volumes when fully released. However, most of his talk, at least that offered to his children or, even more rarely, to me, was delivered in a willfully restrained tenor. The staccato rapidity of his speech recalled the actor James Cagney, in his gangland roles. More than anybody else I have heard before or since, Mr. Conley punctuated his speech with cursing, none of it, so far as I can remember, sexual in its reference. All declarations began with *"Jesus Christ!"* spoken in a descending whine. His wife and children were alternately "dummies," "jackasses," "sons of bitches," or simply "bitches." It cannot be literally true, but it seemed to me that whenever I was playing at the Conleys' at the hour when Mr. Conley came home from work, he would enter the front hall (greeting no one) and walk directly over to a highly polished sideboard in the dining room and inspect it closely, as if looking desperately for an important clue. It would not take him long to find what he was looking for. He would wheel around, incline his head, so as to reach the second-floor rooms, or as far into Creation as he could get, and bellow:

73

"Jesus Christ! There's a new nick in the buffet! Where's the goddamned son of a bitch who's ruining the goddamned son of a bitching buffet?" Kevin could imitate perfectly these and other epithets of his father's. But by no means did he— or anybody who knew him—take his father lightly. Mr. Conley would be terrifying, and my own first impulse was always to avoid any possible contact with him. But he was not quite aversive. There was something undeniably fascinating about someone who lived at such a sustained pitch of outrage and tension. No one ever said of Francis Conley that his bark was worse than his bite. One assumed that, like his bark, his bite would be terrible. The fact of the matter, though, was that one tended to have only oblique encounters with Mr. Conley: a few vituperative seconds framed in a doorway before he slammed the door; end-of-his-rope curses streaming behind him as he ascended or descended the stairs. He was always moving and getting out, slamming the door. A stock movement of his, rather like some highly ritualized bit of animal behavior, was an arc described by his furious tread between the Conleys (slammed) front door and the garage, one meticulously kept half of which was given over to his gleaming yellow Mercury. He would move along this arc of perhaps twenty-five or thirty yards emitting, between the slam of the front door and the slam of the Mercury's door, a continuous stream of reedy profanities, audible as "*J*esus Chri . . . *Son* of a bitchin . . . god*damned* . . . son of a bitchin . . . buffet . . . stinking *fil*thy . . . *son* of a bitch . . . ."

It did not take much—in fact it took nothing—to trigger Mr. Conley's rage. But more than anything or anybody else, his son, Kevin, seemed to epitomize all that had gone wrong. Kevin was a passionate and strong-willed boy. His behavior could be provocative. He seemed maddeningly impervious to reprimand. But these were not the things that seemed to

74

summon up Mr. Conley's invective. It seemed, rather, that the very sight—the fact—of Kevin was the problem: Kevin coasting dreamily down the driveway on his bike, Kevin distractedly pounding his fist into the pocket of his baseball glove, Kevin lying prone on the living room carpet lost in the newspaper comic strips. "What the hell are you two jackasses doing?" he would say to us if, inadvertently, our paths crossed in the house. Once, very uncharacteristically, he sat down at the kitchen table as Kevin and I were finishing our lunch. Naturally conversation stopped abruptly. As Kevin began to drink down a tall glass of milk, his father said:

"Jesus Christ! Will you look at him? *Look* at the son of a bitch. He's not even *drinking* the goddamned milk. He's pouring it down. Not even *tasting it,* for Christ's sake." Mr. Conley got up and stood dramatically, arms folded across his chest. Kevin stopped drinking the milk and looked up into his father's eyes.

"Go ahead, pour it down your throat, you half-wit son of a *bitch*," said Mr. Conley and left the kitchen. The front door slammed. A moment later a car door slammed. Kevin poured another glass of milk and drank it off.

Clearly Kevin had come to terms with his father and with his father's furious approach to life. But the experience was new to me and very important. Up to that point whatever fury I had experienced had been, within the limits of my understanding, caused. The idea of uncaused, free-floating wrath was unsettling, but it also stirred something deep in my recollection; it had the feeling of something true. Caused wrath was a civilized idea, uncaused wrath was more ancient, not an "idea" at all.

One bright blue August afternoon I remember emerging with Kevin out of the high, bleached grass of the field abutting the Conleys' yard. Something was wrong. There was a tangle, a commotion, and it seemed to come down out

75

of the air. The sun was very bright overhead, and we had to shade our eyes and squint to see what was going on. It was Mr. Conley. He had for some reason come out onto a ballustraded second-floor deck to the rear of one of the bedrooms. His arms were flailing in what looked like throwing motions. He was cursing with even more vehemence than usual: "These *god*damned . . . all over the goddamned *house* . . . son of a bitching *mar*bles . . ."

"He's throwing away my marbles," Kevin said, unbelieving, then, "Hey, Dad, what are you doing? Don't! You're throwing away my marbles!"

Kevin had a large, various, impressive collection: regular-size marbles with "cat's eyes" or with a wavery strip or color embedded in the orb. There were also many outsize marbles, some clear, and some stained through with gem colors: cranberry reds, sapphire blues, rich bottle greens. Kevin had amassed two or three shoe boxes full of these, and in our play they could be transformed into anything: soldiers, money, planets, or the gems they so nearly resembled.

There was no stopping Mr. Conley. Up against the wall of the house Kevin stood speechless, craning to see his father overhead casting the marbles, one, two, three at a time out over the yard in the direction of the field. A reason of some kind was offered later—Kevin's room had not been cleaned up, a new nick, perhaps, in the buffet—but I have forgotten what it was. The fact of the matter was that there was Fury in the world. It was magnificent, malignant, and never far away, even on the sunniest afternoons. It knew how to hurt you, knew what you treasured. Kevin and I spent hours, probing long into the firefly-speckled dusk, retrieving what marbles we could out of the tall grasses. We found about twenty.

Was this an unfortunate, too cruel thing for Kevin or, more indirectly, me, to have experienced? I don't think so. It was always stimulating, a little exhilarating to confront Mr. Conley in one of his rages. There was fear bordering on pain, and there was real resentment, too, resentment always swallowed. But to have faced Mr. Conley and to have endured him was important. He not only provided a storehouse of shared, amazing experiences for Kevin and me, he also prepared us for invective, scorn, threats, and unexpected deprivations to come. A world devoid of Mr. Conleys is not, for me, imaginable. Without question the world of history is not devoid of Mr. Conleys.

Which is not to say that Mr. Conley served only to teach lessons, that he could not really hurt you. He could hurt, and sometimes he did. He always seemed to be more or less neutralized when he stood energetically opposed to the other members of his family, including Mrs. Conley. Occasionally, however, both parents, and perhaps some of the girls, would join together in anger at Kevin. When this happened, Mr. Conley's invective carried special weight.

On one such occasion, caused by some unwelcome roughhousing between Kevin and his youngest sister, Kevin was locked out of the house. He seemed undaunted, even a bit elevated by this status when I came to call on him after breakfast. Sitting Indian-style on the cool concrete of his front stoop as he explained the morning's events to me, he seemed to be more the jailer of the other Conleys than the victim of their banishment. He demonstrated his situation to me by taking me around his house to try all possible entrances, all locked.

"Can I come in?" Kevin hollered into the screens of the second-floor rooms.

"You certainly can not!" came Mrs. Conley's shrill reply.

"No, never. Stay out. *Nyah-ah!*" exulted his sisters. From deeper within could be heard a reedy but muffled "*stink*ing son of a bitch can stay there . . ."

77

There it was.

As the sun rose higher over the morning we became lost in play. Kevin pointed out to me the transforming qualities of shadows. Not only did they elongate your image and thrust it back at a rakish angle, but they also—and this was the interesting part—showed your *attitude* for what it really was. Kevin demonstrated this to me by inviting me to look at the shadow play as he performed several different types of runs. He ran across the sunny lawn in the manner of a Scared Child. Then he ran a similar course as a Bully, then as Tarzan. He was right about the shadows. The Scared Child was all tentative darting and halting, The Bully plodded thickly over the turf. Tarzan was fluid and astonishingly swift. He seemed somehow, perhaps because of the way Kevin held up his elbows as he ran, to take flight. Kevin himself was pleased with the effect of Tarzan's shadow. He re-created it several times, stealing looks over his shoulder at the slanting shadow figure cutting a dark edge against the yellow-green grass. Kevin's circuits as Tarzan grew wider and wider, encompassing the front lawns of several neighbors. It was on one of these circuits, flying, that, eyes over his shoulder, Kevin ran full speed, sickeningly, into the sharp edge of a neighbor's For Sale sign.

I didn't see the actual collision because I was looking at his shadow. I heard the clank, then a moan. By the time I looked up, Kevin was whimpering in short gasps and holding up a badly cut arm. It was the first real injury I had seen. Within seconds Kevin's upper body seemed to be covered with blood. From a gash on his forehead, blood poured down into an eye socket and down his cheek. From another cut across his clavicle, blood ran down his front like paint. He was most concerned about his arm where the cut, a deep one, sliced across the muscle of his forearm. "Let me have your belt," he whimpered, but paid no attention to me, instead

78

taking off his own belt clumsily with one hand, then drawing it tight around his arm above the elbow. Doing that—*doing something to an injured part*—was unwatchable for me, disgusting. Holding up his cut arm by the end of his belt, he limped shakily back to his front door where he screamed to be let in.

"You stay out there, Kevin Conley," said Mrs. Conley from one of the upstairs rooms.

"I'm hurt," whimpered Kevin.

"Kevin's hurt!" I screamed.

"Um-hmm, oh *yeah,* oh *sure,*" said his sisters.

"Please," cried Kevin, his voice breaking into a rattle.

This went on and on. At one point Mrs. Conley, practiced in resisting Kevin's ruses, made a show of shutting the upstairs windows so we would no longer be heard. Kevin lay now in a fetal ball on the front stoop, squeezing his upper arm and bleeding onto the mat. "Ring the bell," he told me. "And keep ringing it until they open up."

This I did, in spite of noises inside and specific threats that made my knees wobble. Time stopped in a loud, ringing terror. If I looked down, I saw the scarlet mess of my friend curled into a sobbing ball on the mat. Behind the great door were the sharp voices and the thumping movements of the Conleys as they deliberated what to do about the doorbell. I wanted the Conleys to open the door, but I was desperately afraid they would and that they would be furious. I thought only of the For Sale sign, the clank it had made on impact, and of the crumpling of Kevin's shadow, now disappeared altogether.

I do not know when Mrs. Conley opened the door, but when she did it was to shriek something poisonous at me. Then she spotted Kevin on the mat, and I ran home.

By mid-afternoon Kevin came to call on me. He was elaborately stitched, bandaged in dazzling white—back in action. Although far more elated than he had been the Sunday morning of his black eye, the resolution at home had followed roughly the same pattern. This time the shame and remorse on his mother's part had been monumental. Her affection, her tenderness for him seemed, so far as he was concerned, unbounded. Kevin was, literally, radiant. He had been wounded. He had a story. *He had almost died.* My parents, the neighborhood, everybody wanted to hear about it. I more than envied him; I wanted to be Kevin Conley.

Beginning when he was about ten, Kevin, already a big boy, began to grow rapidly. His new size, and the new possibilities it opened up to him, intensified to the point of straining certain themes in his relationship to me. If Kevin was an especially tall and rangy ten, I was an especially small and slight seven. Although never really a bully, he could not resist dramatizing the sheer fact of his power over me. He would take great pains building my proficiency in games and sports he liked—especially baseball at which, thanks to him I became precociously skilled. Kevin himself was a superb player, a pitcher, and as a young man nearly made a career in professional baseball. He needed, however, to demonstrate his prowess in ways that sometimes seemed to diminish me to the point of disappearance. In the course of pitching batting practice to me, for example, he would—predictably at the point when I had solidly connected to two or three pitches in a row—fire a few pitches by me at such unnerving speed that my arms felt like jelly as I held up the bat. This gesture on his part said: "There is a level, a dimension, of baseball you can never play; it belongs to Kevin Conley and not to you." Similarly, he would spend a twilight hour after supper hitting me fly balls in a vacant lot; but one in, perhaps, every thirty, would be hit impossibly far over my head, occasioning a long, troubled run after the ball.

In foot speed, too, in the strength of his arms, and in the range of his invention, he liked to demonstrate the gap between us. He won decisively all the games we played, but he would often give me special advantages—extra kings in checkers, extra money in Monopoly—to prolong his winning. Kevin was transported by competition of any kind and achieved a visible ecstasy in victory. People like Kevin Conley, I believe, are designed for high drama, others not. He was the kind of player who invariably *did* hit the long ball with the bases loaded to save the game. Many, many times I watched through the fence as he fired a smacking third strike past the last dangerous batter.

For Kevin any game was a treat, but an embellished game was better still. I remember one rainy afternoon spent in his room where, I am sure, both of us passed out of ordinary time. We were playing Monopoly, richly, greedily transported by its complexities, by its gratifying rewards for prudence, by its dumb luck ("Go directly to jail," "Take a ride on the Reading"). Everything about the game combined to overpower sensibility: the warm colors of the properties— the emerald green of Pennsylvania, the crimson of Indiana, the sun-yellow of Marvin Gardens, the deep, rich blue of Boardwalk—the giddy thrill of ownership, of acquiring a *monopoly,* of placing houses and hotels on properties so that when a rival's token landed there, he would have to give up a (perhaps) ruinous fortune in yellow hundred-dollar bills and in orange five-hundred-dollar bills. The best games were those in which near ruin, restoration, and sudden fortune alternated in almost sickeningly succession. It was possible to have *so much*—then a minute later, stunned, eyes stinging a little, to have to give up everything.

Midway through an especially cathartic game, Kevin introduced the idea of suspending the rule that limited to one the number of hotels that could be placed on any property.

81

In the new scheme there could be infinite construction (out of a set of small plastic blocks that fastened together in any direction) and correspondingly colossal "rents" to be paid if one happened to land on a fantastically built-up property. A new, inflated monetary system had to be devised to accommodate the exponentially expanded scale of the game. Now millions and billions of dollars were being exchanged until the hugeness of the amounts melded into a single dizzying concept of Fortune. I lost track of the amounts I owed and the amounts owed to me. And of course I lost the game. But then I lost every game. However, this afternoon I was intoxicated with the realization that the possibilities—the story—of a game could transcend the limitations of ordinary experience and that, better still, the game itself could with special vision be elaborated into a greater game, and *there was no end to it.*

Kevin's growth spurt at ten perhaps hastened the inevitable. He was becoming very hard on me. But playing with other boys closer to me in age and size seemed dishearteningly slow and mechanical. Increasingly I engaged in this lesser life, impatient and ornery if, Kevin-like, I could not transform it a little. Sometimes Kevin would include me in pick-up sports with older friends of his. This was always stimulating, but in that setting my status was narrowly circumscribed: I was to be an "extra" player on Kevin's side, a diminutive sidekick, a "little Kevin" to Kevin. (In this regard I have always felt I understood perfectly Tinkerbell's relationship to Peter Pan.)

This increasingly intolerable relationship came to a head in the course of one such Older Boys softball game in the schoolyard park. Our side was batting, and when I took my turn at the plate, Kevin had volunteered to catch. In a way I always found pleasing, the rival pitcher and his fielders were making much of me, mock-warning each other to back up, as this "little kid" could really hit. The mood was more good-natured than condescending. It was a soft, late summer afternoon, and it seemed to me that the moment held something profoundly sweet. The pitch floated toward me in an agreeable arc, and as I strode forward to hit it, something quick and subliminally familiar moved in my peripheral vision. What it was, had I allowed myself to take it in, was Kevin executing one of his most spectacular, but foolish, tricks. He liked, sometimes, to bolt up out of the catcher's crouch, run around the batter, and intercept the pitch before it could be hit. Perhaps this time he was a bit late getting started, or perhaps something within me refused to acknowledge the stunt. In the event, I swung the bat fully around into the back of Kevin's head. The impact was sharp, horrible in the instant of its realization, and oddly *like* hitting a heavy ball. Kevin fell forward on his face, a dead weight. The other boys ran to attend him. Everyone asked if he was all right. Kevin moaned the word "oh" over and over. Somebody looked at me and said, "It was an accident." Someone else ran to Kevin's house to get help.

By the time help (an hysterical Mrs. Conley) arrived, I had become disoriented and very upset. Kevin was now talking, but he said his whole head hurt very badly. He said he felt as if his head were broken. In my mind's eye the bat kept cracking into the back of Kevin's head, which, I was certain *was* broken. Clearly visible beneath the matted blond hair at the back of his head was an ugly risen ridge of blue-black. It was not a "bump" or an "egg," head injuries with which I was familiar. The raised ridge curved all the way around the back of his head.

"Why did you have to swing?" murmured Kevin, his lips touching the dirt of the base path where he lay.

Suddenly Mrs. Conley was among us.

"What happened? What happened to *Kevin*?" Then to me, "Did you do this to him? *Did you want to kill him?*"

I do not remember how I got home, but I know there was a protracted, irritated plan to get Kevin into a doctor's care. I don't think I ever thought Kevin would die; I did not feel as if I had killed him. He would, I felt, have to be killed frontally. He should not have run around me from behind. He should have let me bat.

Nor was I aware at the time that this richest, this most educative of friendships had come to an end. As it happened Kevin was actually forbidden to play with me, although this is not a restriction he would have honored. Even before I fractured his skull, Kevin had grown into spheres of experience unknowable to me. And in the years to follow we became mutually alien, although never unfriendly.

Years later when he was a senior in high school, and I was a sophomore, we became reacquainted. The new relationship was agreeable, but for reasons I could not understand, oddly restrained. Two "coincidences" had reunited us: we began at approximately the same time to date sisters, and we each took summer jobs keeping the grounds of the same cemetery. But there was nothing stirring or magical in the reunion, although we spent many pleasant hours pottering around the warm, windy acres of gravestones. We compared openly our experiences of the sisters, even "double-dated" a few times, but this relative intimacy belonged to the intelligible "civic" world I was just, at sixteen, beginning to arrange for myself.

Only once, and then memorably, did the teenage world we shared come into conjunction with the world of our boyhood. It happened late one warm summer night. We had just dropped off the sisters at their house and decided to find someplace to get a hamburger. Kevin's car was low on gas, so we drove to his house to get some money. As we approached the Conley house, something seemed out of order. Kevin stopped the car along the tree lawn, but neither of us got out.

Although it was past midnight, every light in the Conley house appeared to be on. Hallway lights, bright kitchen lights, the porch lights—even the upstairs bedroom windows were beacons of yellow-white light. The front and side doors of the house stood open, creating great archways of light. I had a strong impression that the house was empty. Then we heard the smashing of glass just out of view, at the garage-end of the house. We got out and moved cautiously up the walk to the foot of the driveway. From the relative darkness we looked up into the brilliant, almost white light of the open garage. On one side, yellow and gleaming, was Mr. Conley's prized Mercury. In the other, vacant stall stood Kevin's father, holding an empty milk bottle in each hand. Unaware of us, he stood for a minute facing the white rear of the garage. Then he raised his right arm and hurled the milk bottle against the wall, where it popped and smashed noisily onto the concrete. A second later he did the same with the bottle in his left hand. Then he walked to the side wall of the garage and picked up two more bottles.

Kevin turned to me, looking aggravated, a little tired. There were two more explosions of glass from the garage, then a reedy, barely audible stream of curses.

Kevin flashed a wide, bright smile. His smile said thank God—to you I don't have to explain anything.

Also from the Lives of the Saints: Cyrus Best

My experiences with Kevin Conley had been alive with spirits. The more accessible spirits were terrible; the remote ones—so remote!—filled me with a longing so deep it was painful. I knew the spirits were true, but I did not know if they thought *I* was true. I was not a Catholic.

I was aware from such experiences as my near drowning, my near imprisonment, and the fracturing of my friend's skull, that significant things would be done to me, and I would do significant things. Moreover, these things were likely, in my case, to be destructive. I seemed to be always helplessly on the verge—or already past it—of crime. How could my parents and my teachers ever understand this? They would caution or reprimand me as if I could willfully set myself to do beneficial tasks or willfully resist an invitation to head out into a tangle of fields at a late hour. I don't think I had a will. I wonder if any boy has.

I felt genuinely responsible for my actions: for no one other than I had batted the stone through the church window, had scratched his name into the veneer of the television set. I longed to strike the pilfered match, longed for the spectacle of the blaze. I was drawn to the silver in my mother's change purse. I could not rest until I beheld its flash, felt its slightly oily clink and heft in my palm. And as I have already said, I yearned to kill every animal that caught my eye. I knew I was bad, and worsening, but I also knew there was nothing in my power that could be done to change my course.

With Catholics it was different. Even when they were worse than I was, they were better. They were always with the spirit, connected to it. They could confess and be clean. My filthiest, heaviest sin would be lifted away from a Catholic like a veil of gauze. Catholics seemed especially disdainful of sin, in an odd hurry to do it all, to get it over with, because they knew they could be pure again, as clean as light. How, I wondered, could I *feel* so Catholic, but have no way out of the world, no way to confess. Another wonderful boyhood friend would show me the way out, a way I never could have guessed.

His name was Cyrus Best, and he was different. My earliest recollection of him is as a strikingly anomalous presence in my third grade classroom. With his spiky hair shaved close all around his great round head, he summoned up something of the prickly animals of storybooks: a hedgehog or a porcupine.

His clothes, too, were unusual. Although we were unaware of it then, most of us came from moderately prosperous households and tended to wear what was stocked in the area's department stores. This was not so with Cyrus. He dressed always in large—possibly even men's—shirts that were worn or laundered to a state of pale gray colorlessness. His trousers were also outsized and shapeless, never blue jeans or corduroys, which were standard, but rather, apparently, the trousers of Sunday suit handed down. Cyrus wore these baggy trousers high over his hips, and he cinched them in tight with a wide black leather belt. The belt was enormous. A hole had been punched so far into its perimeter that when Cyrus buckled it, there was as much belt strap hanging free as there was around his waist. He wore, in all seasons, a great pair of heavy boots that laced up over the ankles and that were made of the same oily-black leather as his belt.

The visual effect of Cyrus standing or seated among his classmates was something like a voided place in the composition. One tended to avert one's eyes, not to see him at all. Then, when one looked closely, there was an impression of camouflage, of, perhaps, a boy-prisoner brought into school, of a boy sprung whole from a faded daguerreotype of Life on the Plains.

Cyrus Best. If he was a void in our classroom, it was because he did not belong in school at all, certainly not in that school. He could not manage any of the schoolwork. The pages he composed, whether written compositions or arithmetic combinations, were always, when I saw them, a jumble of blotches, scratchy marks, and failed erasures. Even at the board he seemed able only to make a mess. Asked to spell or to recite, he stumbled or froze. There were painful attempts by the teacher to stop him from saying "ain't." "It's correct to say 'is not' or 'isn't,' 'are not' or 'aren't,' but 'ain't' is incorrect."

"How come?" Cyrus asked once.

"Because 'ain't' is not a word. It's slang."

"Who says? You know what it means."

"That's just the way it is. It is not correct to say 'ain't.' " She added hurtfully, "It is considered ignorant to say 'ain't.' "

"Well, I'm ignorant," said Cyrus, one of the only classroom assertions I can remember him making in our several years of schooling in common. When I got to know him better I realized he was not being insolent in making such a remark; he was defending his family, all of whom said "ain't." They also said "warsh" for "wash," "ruff" for "roof," and "dint" for "didn't."

I was impressed that Cyrus, although unable to carry the linguistic point, somehow got the psychological better of our teacher in this encounter. For a minute the rules of usage seemed to flap fussily over our heads and then, somehow, to blow away. Cyrus, by contrast, held his ground. He would be corrected for it, marked down for it, but the fact of the matter is that he said "ain't." Ain't was perfect for Cyrus, and we knew what he meant.

While at cross-purposes with practically all the business of school, Cyrus was a substantial and deeply serious person. His conviction carried a weight I had not yet experienced in either a child or an adult. He was in some ways the most adult person I knew. At certain moments he seemed to be so old, so heavy with time and experience, that he was no age at all.

I never knew precisely where Cyrus came from, but I know he came from the land. Later, when I knew him better, he explained that "his people" came from downstate, "down along the river." *His people*—the idea of descending from A People awed me. The idea also helped to explain Cyrus's spiritual distance from other children—and also the way he looked. When I met his mother and father and three of his many older brothers, the concept of Cyrus's People was confirmed. Although different enough in their individual features, they were startlingly similar in essentials. All the Bests, excepting Cyrus, were tall, large and sharp of bone, and, without being actually skinny, gave the impression of emaciation. Their eyes were far recessed beneath their bony brows. Below the eye their cheekbones stood out as prominently as elbows, the effect of which was to further recess the eye and to create great shadowy hollows beneath cheekbone and jaw. Bones—the Bests were all bones. Mrs. Best's ankles emerged out of the muscular base of her calf like an upended Sierra, sharp as a knife along the ridge of its peak. The wrists of Cyrus's grown brothers, Len, Carol, and K.C., were as broad as spatulas, the hinge-ends bulbous as stones. But looking at the Bests I did not see "ankles" or "wrists"; I saw bones. I could imagine the wind-washed thighbones, skulls, and pelvises of the Bests bleaching in a wilderness, a world of steers and bison, coyotes and vultures.

The Bests—and possibly all their People—had the same color eyes. Cyrus said it was gray, but it was not gray. It was, rather, an infinitely variable shade of khaki: honey-gold at the darkest, pale wheat at the lightest. Cyrus's eyes, especially outside in the bright daylight of the fields, could become so pale, so light, that, looking at him, he seemed to cease looking back at you. I felt at those times as if I were looking not at Cyrus, but through him, through him into the fields themselves, but into a vaster, older expanse of fields. Cyrus did go into trances, and when he did, the wind seemed to blow right through him.

The Bests were poor. Cyrus had declared this to me the first time I went over to his house. As we walked up the wooden steps to his front porch he said, "My people are poor." If he had not provided the word, I still would have gotten the sense of it.

The inside of Cyrus's house smelled of the past. Whatever was going to happen in that house had already happened. Even in the summer the house was unnaturally cool, dark, and damp. The heavy air smelled of must and of something uncomfortably sweet. There seemed to be almost nothing in the rooms—a single stuffed chair in one room, a wobbly wooden table in another. The basement, where we often found ourselves, had a floor of earth, and was as rich in possibilities as a cave. Once in this basement, Cyrus told me, a black rat "bigger'n a dog" had come up out of a basketful of laundry and had walked wobbily right at him. Cyrus had hollered for his brother, Len, who came down the stairs with his .22, put it to the rat's head, and dispatched it.

Up at the top of the house, under the eaves, was a closet full of old sheets and rags: "Fulla mice," Cyrus said, and it was. For me and I think for Cyrus too, his house was, for a time, a dream come true: a place to hunt *inside*.

Cyrus understood my urge to hunt and to some extent shared it. But unlike Kevin Conley, he had a steely, inviolable sense of what was allowable and what was not. Unlike me, he had a will. Even though, for example, his brothers owned, among them, the arsenal of my dreams—.22 rifles, shotguns, pellet guns, air pistols—we never so much as picked up one of their guns, even to handle. Cyrus would not let me. The guns were his brothers' Property. Furthermore, he knew that my parents had forbidden me to play with guns. Commandments like these were law to him. I was amazed. How had this happened? How had Cyrus come to be this way?

One breezy, private morning he told me. Perhaps the phenomenon is not limited to children, but a surprising transformation of locale seems the surest catalyst to deep personal revelations. Thus children tell their truest stories and most fearful secrets when they have just crawled inside a tree house or when they have beached their rowboat on an uninhabited island mid-river. The site of Cyrus's revelation to me was, simultaneously, the sunny recess of an attic dormer (adjacent to the mouse closet) and a commodious limb of an elm tree, which veered upward in a sharp ell just a foot or two from the dormer window. By climbing, one of us, up to the limb and by the other of us raising the dormer window, we could converse just as naturally as if a bone-breaking drop of twenty feet did not exist between us.

"I ain't told you this before," Cyrus began, "but I'm saved."

Saved. It was a charged word. Before Cyrus explained anything, I knew exactly what he meant. Something important had happened to Cyrus, something as important as a great wound, as death. It had happened through his church, and he had had to give up everything to get it. Now everything began to make sense about Cyrus: his punishing haircuts, his no-color clothes, the lost-lightness of his eyes, his being poor. This was deep, was infinitely more real than being Catholic. The marvels of Catholicism seemed to float about in the air like the ascending spirit of Daddy Mac, like the fine, subtle thing that happened to the holy sacrament at the instant the priest blessed it. The promise of Catholicism was everywhere outside you and around you—real and sweet, but external. Cyrus's message was in himself, *was* himself. The thing had already happened, and he could explain it to me, beautifully, from his perch in the tree.

Cyrus was a Baptist. I could think of no Baptist church in our town—although I thought I knew all of the churches—but it didn't matter. I knew the story of John the Baptist, and that was satisfying enough. The idea of John the Baptist fit in with Cyrus's people. Both came from "down along the river" and were most vividly imaginable there. In my mind, John had stood in the cleanest, bakingest heat. The river just behind him was cold and terrifying and final. Cyrus had himself been baptized only a year or so earlier. "I had to want it," he explained. A Baptist preacher had picked him up with all his clothes on and had submerged him in a deep pool, a deep pool right in the Baptist church, until, in Cyrus's words, "I near drown't."

Cyrus emerged from his baptism saved. "I knew when I was under," he said, "that I was givin' up everything. I dint care if I died, I was through with the bad. That's when God saved me." I knew exactly what he meant. I remembered my own submersion down through the tans and browns of the Wisconsin lake. I had—I thought, perhaps—been *preparing* for it in my prayer, when I was hauled abruptly up to the surface. But it had not been completed, had not happened to me. I had not been saved.

Cyrus told me what it meant to "give up the bad." Baptists did not drink and did not smoke. Nor, I thought, would I. Baptists did not dance. This gave me pause. Dancing to me meant the fantastically artificial movements choreographed for the television variety shows we watched on Sunday nights. I supposed the clickety-click of tap dancing also counted as dancing. The only other dancing I could think of was the kind I observed at the school dances of the junior high and high school kids: the swirl of full skirts and the fast, prissy stepping of saddle shoes and white socks. It was hard for me to see the sin in this—in fact I did not see it—but I accepted it on faith from Cyrus.

"Having a dirty mind"—that is, not having one—was the key. You had to concentrate not to think of your naked body and of other people's naked bodies all the time. This I understood. "Otherwise," Cyrus said, "you'll get the sex feeling." This I did not understand; I did not think of sex yet as a feeling. I thought of it as a very personal, inherently embarrassing word. I determined that sex encompassed everything to do with naked bodies, and that they could somehow lure you into fiery hell. "You can't fight it some-

94

times," Cyrus said almost sadly. "It just gets to you, unless you have God's help. It was starting to get to me before I was saved."

Suddenly and terrifyingly, I felt it starting to get to me. Isolated as I was aloft in Cyrus's attic, frontally naked bodies, pink and pulsing, kept crowding into my imagination. Hell was becoming fleshy, alive with feeling, personal.

Cyrus, although just a year older than I was, had thought a great deal about sex. He had a special, highly developed sense of it. He told me the Millers, his next door neighbors, were going to hell for their sex. I knew Freddy Miller, a cheerful, loudmouthed boy several years older than I was, and there was a sister, Linda, older still. "They're naked near all the time," Cyrus said. He was not an exaggerator, and I knew what a surveillant he could be. "They're naked together, all of them, the whole family." I never looked Freddy Miller in the face again.

One bitterly leafless day in late autumn, Cyrus and I struck out after school for the fields. We had no clear aim in view: to scare up a pheasant or some rabbits, to find something worth saving. At the point where the paved road gave way to a double-rutted dirt path, Cyrus pinched my sleeve and froze. Up ahead of us about a quarter of a mile walked two girls. They wore bright windbreakers, and their heads were bound with scarves. I knew them both. They were girls from the fifth grade, and I rather liked one of them, a dark-haired girl named Joan. The other was named Priscilla. "I see what they're up to," said Cyrus. He was very tense.

"Those *girls?* Priscilla and Joan? What could they do?"

"I seen them before," Cyrus said quietly.

We followed the girls, at a distance, along the tractor path. A mile or so into the fields they cut off into the high grass. We cut in too, where we were, and began angling cautiously, finally on all fours, in the direction we imagined

95

the girls had taken. It was very cold. I wondered what Cyrus had in mind. He was neither a joker nor a fighter—and he would never hurt a girl.

"What are we doing?" I asked him.

"We're going to see this," he said cryptically. He was extremely agitated. He was trembling.

Again Cyrus pinched my sleeve. He had spotted the girls just ahead. Unconnected fragments of their talk rode the sharp wind in our direction. Cyrus and I lay still on our bellies for a minute or two, then we began inching forward in the direction of the girls. When we got to within twenty yards of them and could hear their talking plainly, we stopped. Parting the grasses we could see them. They were facing each other, sitting Indian style, unaware of us. Something about them transfixed Cyrus. He seemed to have become disengaged. He was tensed for something monumental, perhaps unbearable.

Joan and Priscilla seemed to have arrived at some sort of agreement. Still facing each other, they adjusted themselves to kneeling positions. Then, despite the cold, they unzipped their jackets, took them off, and laid them aside. They looked directly into each other's faces without speaking. Cyrus was right; some deep, forbidden ritual was about to take place. The anticipation of it was almost painful. Still without speaking, still facing each other, the girls extended their arms to each other and clasped hands. They knelt in this position and looked into one another's eyes until I could stand it no more.

I stood up and screamed, "Hey, Joan! Hey, Priscilla!— Boo!"

It was spoiled. Badly startled, they recognized us quickly and turned away. I attempted some teasing, some banter. I wanted desperately to banish every trace of the

96

primitive, oddly magnetic spell that had been cast by the girls a moment earlier.

"Why don't you go away," said Joan. "Leave us alone." They put their jackets back on and made their way back to the path. We allowed them some distance, then followed.

All the chilling walk back to town Cyrus did not say a word. Only when we parted at his door did he speak.

"I wish I never seen it." He looked tortured. "But it keeps happening, everywhere I go. I'm going to pray God to help me to forget it."

Not that winter, but months later in the crystal clarity of a gusty June morning, Cyrus taught me to pray. He did not teach me specific words to say, for which I am still grateful. He convinced me that prayer was real. He helped me to start.

I always liked to hear about Cyrus's religious ideas and about his praying, but this was different. I was no Baptist.

"It don't matter," Cyrus said. "Don't worry about it. Give up worryin' about how it's going to be. Just give up and pray."

I wanted to, but I balked.

"God will hear you. He hears everything you say," Cyrus continued. And then, as if prying open a capsule or a nut which had, unbeknownst to me, been confining me from all the sunburst wonders of the waking world, he said, simply, "God's right here."

And it was true. Cyrus and I were sitting at the foot of a colossal elm at the edge of a town park. The exposed roots of the elm radiated away from its base to form adjacent, boy-size alcoves. The great elm held us securely between the sweet green earth and the infinite blue and muslin of the sky. The sky was alive that morning. Billowing cumulus clouds the size of continents opened up and multiplied against the blue. A thought would bring on the wind, and the wind would bring on a thought. And the instant Cyrus said "God's right here," a gust swept past us, through us, flattening our hair, hissing through the hedges, raising a deafening whoosh in the branches straining overhead. Now, in this noise, was the time. In air so clean, beneath a sky so vast, here in the wind, moving with all this movement I could pray. "God," I said, "I love you."

I was so happy. Something was lost—what? It was myself. Everything I was, everything I thought I had made of myself was gone, behind me, blown away with the wind. I was simply aware, watching myself at the base of the tree, as if from high in the sky, that it had happened. It had finally happened. I was nine years old, barely awake, unschooled, undisciplined, far, far from good, but this great connectedness, this opening up had happened.

It would not, I am sure, have happened without Cyrus. Cyrus did not create the moment any more than he created the wind. Nor did Cyrus create this God, for God was no longer the God of Cyrus's stories, the God of the Baptists. This was God the Immanent. Cyrus did not make him, but Cyrus made him real. Cyrus did the simplest thing: he pointed God out.

An experience of the Presence makes one feel infinitely glad and grateful in its afterglow. But the emotional pitch does not last, nor can one re-create it at will. Nor, again, does the experience by itself advance one in the direction of goodness. There is a newly heightened awareness of how *far* from God one can be, and this is my understanding of what "badness" is. But the desolation of being far from God, does not drive one back to the Presence. The Prodigal Son was not typical. In fact he was practically unprecedented; Jesus had to *introduce him* as an idea. And even in the parable, he, the son, did not expect much when he decided to go back home: he looked only for a living less demeaning than being an outcast tender of pigs. The surprising character in the parable is, of course, the father. He represents the Presence. He is love unexpected, love unearned. There would be no parable if the son had thought: "Enough of this eating pig scraps. I know the kind of man Father is—he'll welcome me back with a feast."

Cyrus had put me in touch with God, into a dialogue that has never ceased for a second. But I did not become a "better" boy. For quite a sustained time I think I became worse. I prayed often, many times a day, but since my initial invocation, I cannot remember any praise or gratitude from that period; I can recall only highly specific petitions. I wanted to perform outstanding feats in games, I wanted to have unlikely, very expensive things, I wanted, above all, to be tall.

I was at this time going through the same developmental transition that had changed Kevin Conley at ten and that had brought an end to our friendship. I had become more than confident; I was cocksure. Schoolwork was effortless, and no one did it faster than I did. I could spell anything, had an answer for everything. I was captain of the playground teams, boss of the anarchic after-school gangs. Games were played on my terms. I threw the passes, I pitched, I batted first. I was completely, unstoppably mobile. On foot or by bicycle I could transport myself anywhere in town or into the fields surrounding it. There was even a clearly worked out plan, in case I needed it, for getting out of the town forever and into the wilderness. I would board one of the commuter trains in town and ride to the end of the line, to Chicago. From there I would haul my bag over the bridge spanning the Chicago River, proceed up one short city block, turn right down a long one, then left again and into the LaSalle Street station where I would board a train for Denver, stow

99

away in the lavatory until the conductors made their rounds. Then I would take a seat in the dome car where, with only a curved shield of glass between me and the clouds, I would cross over the Mississippi and ride screaming over the plains toward the Rockies.

In the wake of so much autonomy Cyrus somehow got lost. I had come to prefer the playground and sports to the prairie and the hunt, and Cyrus belonged to the prairie. I had also come to care about how I looked and what I wore, and in this dimension of life Cyrus failed even to register. He either could not do or did not want to do the things I did, and my own course had become unalterable. I continued to see him as a superior being, a heavy fixture, a boulder, in the classroom. The drab flags of his clothing reminded me of something important. He stood for the God-sense, and as long as he had it, I could, when I chose, have it too.

Late one afternoon when I was rummaging around our cellar just before dinner, I discovered in an old chest a wooden box containing small ornamental pistols. The trunk was full of oddments that had belonged to my grandfather, who had died the year before. His things were temporarily in the cellar awaiting distribution. A year earlier, when I was still under the sway of the hunt, the pistols would have appeared to me as irresistible, a message from the mythic world. The pistols still interested me, but in a dulled, confusing way. Replacing the others carefully in their velvet-lined box, I took one and slipped it into my pocket. After dinner, alone in my bedroom, I inspected the pistol closely. It had a worn, pearly handle, and although no more than a few inches long, it had an appealing heft to it. Its oiled steel barrel rotated pleasingly, one click at a time. *This is valuable,* it occurred to me, *and I am going to steal it*. But of course I had stolen it already.

The pistol was important. In fact, it seemed in its beauty

to have a kind of power over me. A year earlier a clear image of what to do with the gun would, I am sure, have presented itself. As it was I felt driven to do something with it, but I did not know what.

The next afternoon I called on the Burnetts, the most loveless, most delinquent boys I knew. I told them I had something to show them. They let me in. The Burnetts were always available, always home. There was something dangerously languid about them and about their dark, untidy house.

"What is this?" Bob Burnett asked, handling the pistol. "a .38?"

"I don't know."

"What are you gonna do with it?"

I didn't know.

"Wanna sell it?"

Yes. Suddenly it was clear. That was the answer: I could rid myself of this upsetting, too significant prize by selling it. I would still be secretly to the good, "ahead" for my theft: I would have money.

Bob Burnett offered me three dollars for it. That was more money than I usually handled, except at Christmas, but it did not seem a large amount. I worried that it was not enough.

"Take it or leave it," said Bob Burnett. "I don't even know if the damn thing works."

That settled it. The last thing I wanted was to keep the gun. It had begun to seem almost alive. When I handed it over, I felt a twinge. It seemed so ancient, so finely made. It did not fit in with the Burnetts. As I walked back home, holding the three folded bills tightly in my palm, I thought about my grandfather. He had owned and at some point cared about that pistol. It had fit into a plan, into a collection, into the same fine European order as his stamps and paints and fountain pens did. That my grandfather's order should be undone by my thievery and that something worthy of my grandfather's care should make its way into the world of the Burnetts made me feel inutterably ashamed. This was not a particular sin, I realized, but *sin itself*. It tugged at me, it bore me along like a current.

The next afternoon I walked into town and spent the three dollars as fast as I could. I bought filled cupcakes, comic books, caps, a bag of plastic combs, baseball cards, candy, and gum. I wanted nothing durable. I wanted to get rid of that money as badly as I had wanted to get rid of the pistol. When I had spent the money, I knew I had squandered away a small excellence. The fact was intolerable.

Perhaps a week later my mother confronted me directly: had I taken one of her father's pistols? There had been four, and now there were three; one was missing. The pistols, she explained seriously (and with heartbreaking kindness), were not playthings; they were real. They could be dangerous. Moreover, they were to go to my uncle. They were valuable. "Did you take one?" she asked me "—to play with?" For some reason, I was convinced she knew everything.

"No," I lied in a loud voice. "What pistol? I didn't know Pops had pistols. Why do you think I have one of his pistols?"

Cyrus had told me once in deep seriousness: *one lie always leads to another one. Once you start, you can't stop.* I could not stop, and I was certain my mother knew it. "You're sure?" she asked me, and let me go.

My father, however, did not let matters like this drop. I had taken the gun, he told me, and now I had to give it back. What was so hard about that? he asked. *One lie led to another.* I was guarded, then elaborately inventive. My father became furious. *"Why can't you tell me the truth?"* I couldn't tell him. I was prepared to take a beating, even to let myself be killed before I would admit my theft or admit my lie. I was in a helpless descent, and I knew I was going to go as far down as it went. Neither my story nor my evasions were the slightest bit convincing, but I knew that I had to stand by them. My nighttime fantasy of flight suddenly started pressing itself into the realm of possibility: I could leave for school in the morning but instead go to the station where I would board a commuter train for the city. There, one block over the bridge, then one block right, then one block left, I would change stations and slip aboard the train to Denver. I could shine shoes. I could get a rifle and hunt. My heart raced because I was really going to have to go.

My father set the following terms: he was going out of town the next night, but when he returned the following night, he wanted the pistol and the straight story about what had happened to it. We would get the story straight, he told me, *if it took all night.* He invited me to "think it over." I was dismissed to my room.

What I thought over was the trains, the change of stations, and Denver. As the possibility of flight became real, I was aware that behind the flickering images—LaSalle Street Station, Denver, the Rockies—was nothing but darkness. *But I was going.* I heard a mounting roar, sensed an opening maw. *But I was going.*

That night I knew that for the first time in my conscious life I did not have the resources to do the next thing. Each time I considered all that happened—the theft of the pistol, its sale, the spending of the proceeds, all my lies, my father's terms—I found myself in an inescapable terror. What if I told the truth—? Where would I even begin? *One lie had led to another.* I could see returning the pistol. That I could do. But the lies—. I had stood by those lies. If I admitted them, I felt I would disappear. Even in my prayers I could not mention the lies. They were what I had made of myself. They were all I was. I wished I were dead.

The next morning I plunged deeper into falseness. I could feel myself moving into a shadowy dimension in which, in return for a measure of calm, one willingly gives up the knowledge of what is real. Before breakfast I went down to the cellar, opened the old trunk, and searched hard for the pistol I had stolen and sold.

That afternoon after school I bicycled over to the Burnetts' and asked for the pistol back. I told them I was not allowed to sell it. My parents wanted it back. The Burnett boys hedged. They seemed used to this kind of thing. "Too bad," said Bob Burnett. "We broke it."

I told them this did not matter. I would take it back anyway. I had to have it. The Burnetts looked at each other.

"It'll cost you three bucks."

Of course it would. Why hadn't I thought of that? I asked them if I could trade them something for the pistol. "Like what—?" I could not think of any of my possessions that would appeal to the Burnetts. I suggested my records, my games. The Burnetts laughed. My allowance was fifty cents a week. I asked if I could buy the gun back over time. That would be six weeks, they said; no. Bob Burnett left the room and then reappeared. He had the pistol. It *was* broken. The pearl was missing from one side of the handle. The pistol was junk. He twirled it around his finger by the trigger guard.

"Cost you three bucks."

I do not remember leaving the Burnetts' house. I remember only being stopped still, straddling the bar of my bicycle, a block or two away from my house. There, seemingly without arriving, was Cyrus Best.

"What's the trouble?"

I told Cyrus what I had done—everything but the lies. I could not admit them to anyone. It was easy to tell Cyrus. He seemed to understand perfectly, even the hardest parts, like needing to sell the pistol and spending the money right away on practically nothing. Cyrus knew the Burnetts. He had watched their gunplay in the fields, heard their foulmouthed talk. They were his enemies. I told Cyrus about the trains and about Denver. I suddenly wanted him to come with me.

"You ain't going to Denver."

He would not come with me. Once again, for my sake as much as for his, I reconstructed what I had done, and once again there was no way out. It was supper time. He told me not to worry, and we parted. That night I slept fitfully.

That morning I awoke utterly listless. The school day passed in a blur. The anticipation of the battle ahead with my father sickened me. I had already decided I would say nothing at all, to wait him out, even if he did stay up with me all night, even if he shook me and hit me. At some point he would give up. I would be left alone. Then I would slip off to the train.

I went straight home after school. Any diversion was unthinkable. Soon after I got home, the doorbell rang. It was Cyrus. It was strange seeing him on our porch. He did not seem to belong in our house, even on our street. His pale, wheat-colored eyes looked straight into mine.

"I want you to take this." He handed me a small, black cloth purse. Inside were two paper dollars and four quarters. "You can pay me back sometime."

I started to say, "What's this for?" But this was not necessary with Cyrus. I knew what it was for. It was for the Burnetts. I also knew that Cyrus had sacrificed something monumental to get hold of three dollars. The gesture made us both very uncomfortable on the porch.

105

"I been prayin' for you," Cyrus said.

I'm a liar, I said to myself, and to Cyrus: "I'll pay you back."

"I gotta go," said Cyrus, relieved to be on his way.

This was the first clear instance of a lesson I would be taught throughout my life. Just at the brink of justice, I would be given love. And love, like the Presence, did not improve me, even when, as in this instance it saved me from worry and pain. Love reflected shiningly back onto its giver, so that, if anything, the distance lengthened between Cyrus and me. Cyrus had never seemed holier; I was still held fast in a tangle of my own lies. The gun was secured and returned, and hard feelings were softened. But I never told my father what had happened to the pistol. Improvement was entirely up to me.

After that afternoon Cyrus truly did disappear. He was made to drop back a grade in school, the equivalent of being deported in shame to a primitive land of one's own past. Our paths ceased to cross, in school or afterward. Several years later, in high school, I had a dim awareness of his being enrolled in the Vocational, as opposed to the College Preparatory, curriculum.

We spoke only one other time, when I was eighteen and he was, it seemed, forty. I had stopped in at the hardware store in town to pick up some paint for my father. Cyrus was working behind the counter. He was a man, not even a young man, and he now featured the great, sharp bones of his People. There was something new, something closed off and finished in his pale eyes. He chatted a little, filled me in, but he made it clear that mixing the paint came first. He and I were alone in the store. He let me know that he was devoted to this work. He told me he had been employed there "regular" all through high school. With a kind of reverence he told me his weekly wage—which was substantial and made Cyrus seem still more remote from me. He was going to run the business, he told me with convincing determination. I took in Cyrus's appearance. He still had a crew cut, but it seemed to have reconciled itself to his head. He wore a clean plaid shirt open at the collar and a pair of sharply creased gabardine pants. He could have been somebody's uncle. Was his spirit still intact, I wondered. Was it somehow guiding him through this emporium of tools, hinges, fasteners, pots and pans, glues, paints, and—I noticed under the glass—pearl-handled knives and pistols. Cyrus belonged to this dimly lit, infinitely complex room. There was something priestly in his movements. As he made my change, with an unusual intensity of concentration, it occurred to me that I had never paid him back the three dollars. I thought of doing it there on the spot, but a stab of the original guilt stopped me short. And I was afraid of something that lay behind Cyrus's empty eyes.

Love and Love's Objects

The gifts of love I experienced as a boy seemed to save me from, or at least to delay, the just consequences of my actions. But this was not really so, nor could it have been so, justice being justice. Love and justice are never opposed, but what boy knows this? It is now perfectly clear to me that experiences of love are not meant to modify the practical circumstances of life; they are meant to illuminate Love itself. This is not to say that love may not move one to good works or to work wonders. But love is as elusive as it is vast. It summons you, not the reverse. It cannot be used, cannot be doled out sensibly, according to a plan. Love can never, strictly speaking, be *therapy*, although in an age of therapy this is an appealing, if hopeless, idea.

Love is the greatest mystery. Psychologists, theologians, and philosophers have stratified love, have overlaid it with categories, so that a mother's love, a friend's, a bride's would be categorically different phenomena. But here common speech and common sense do well to muddy the waters. Love is love. If love has many faces, we should treasure every one.

Easiest to treasure is love's most beautiful face: romantic love. It is an infinitely renewable story. We find ourselves playing our helpless, ecstatic parts before we are aware we are doing it. Falling in love has no beginning; it has always already begun. No one has to tell us "this is love" or "the prince is in love with the princess." We know. Perhaps we ourselves were conceived by lovers in love. Perhaps we awoke to life among lovers in love. But whatever the case, when the time comes for us, we recognize it. I myself recognized it definitively when I was four. My gaze came to rest on the glossy cover of a record album. The record was the Oscar Strauss operetta, *The Chocolate Soldier,* and the cover photograph showed two lovers (Nelson Eddy and Risë Stevens) loosely embracing, looking lovingly into each other's eyes. The photograph was tinted in browns and golds, so that the lovers' faces looked as if they were subtly bronzed. Their smooth skin, their fingertips, their very adoration seemed everlasting.

The soldier was immaculate in a dark tunic with a stiff, standing collar. Gold braid crossed his chest. His blond hair, combed wavily back from a high forehead, was almost distractingly beautiful. All the lines of his face—the sheer nose, the sharp line of his upper lip, the strong jaw—cohered. He was very handsome. His lady was perfect. A bright light shone down onto her face, so that her long, plaited hair seemed itself alight. She looked up into his eyes, he down into hers. Her lips were dark and full as fruit. So mutual, so charged, so bronzed over with love were the Chocolate Soldier and his lady that in a way impossible to describe they looked exactly alike.

110

In the light of that cover photograph, the score of *The Chocolate Soldier* has always been for me the ultimate love story. Through its songs (I have never seen the whole production performed, nor read the Shaw play on which it is based) it is clear that the characters are detached from everything else in the world except their love for each other. Everything but love is insubstantial and silly—he is a *chocolate* soldier. And out of the infinite strands of the world's silliness, out of nothing, lovers can embroider bits of love, can make music out of it as pretty as the harmonic tinkling of glass. The soldier sings:

> I am just a chocolate soldier man,
> For me you feel great pity,
> Just a funny chocolate soldier man
> In a uniform so pretty

She answers:

> . . . a silly chocolate soldier man
> Just made to please your misses

He agrees:

> So sweet, might melt
> If 'ere they felt
> A full-grown maiden's kisses.

They tease and play, grow deeply, sweetly sad, love again, have each other in love forever. At one point (to my four-year-old understanding) the soldier's lady seems to have died, and through a night of sadness that is in no way hopeless but, rather, thickly suffused with love recalled, the soldier sings a ballad. In it he says that while the moon is shining, its shining is unnecessary "while my lady sleeps." I realized that the soldier must have been outdoors all night in a garden, in moonlight, in love, and the yearning I felt to be lost in love in silvery light is like nothing I have ever felt before. I can feel it now.

The climax of the story is an ascendingly tonic declaration of love and betrothal, the duet "My Hero." It must be the most openhearted, absolutely final declaration of love ever composed. In my own mental scheme of it, the chocolate soldier and his lady ascend, singing, up into a celestial marriage of blinding light.

Before I reached school age I had played *The Chocolate Soldier* until it was barely audible. My parents were pleased enough to indulge what must have seemed to them a highly specific taste. I wonder now whether my passion for *The Chocolate Soldier* did not perhaps stir my parents' own romantic impulses. After all, this was the music of *their* early childhood, out of vogue for decades. In any event, I was generously provided with recordings of other operettas: *The Student Prince, The Merry Widow, Desert Song, Rose Marie*. To my amazement and deep satisfaction, *all of them* produced the love feeling. All of the heroines were, like the chocolate soldier's lady, beautiful, each only incidentally, even randomly, holding a place in the practical world. (In *Student Prince* Cathy is a Heidelberg barmaid, but she is inherently regal and ranks, by love's code, with the student prince.) The heroes were all like the chocolate soldier. The uniform and rank of the student princes, French legionnaires, and Canadian Mounties were, I sensed, the necessary plumage of romance. They embellished life's central business, which was to assume the ancient attitutes of love.

None of my neighborhood friends—and I might add, none of my friends since—showed the slightest interest in or comprehension of what, I felt, the operettas had to say. This did not matter much. I was happy for the stories to speak only to me. But I needed to answer. In remote patches of lawn and park, the wind in my hair, I sang. I sang "Indian Love Call," "Golden Days," "While My Lady Sleeps." It was the beginning of a continuing lifetime of very loud singing.

Most transporting of all the love songs, however, was "Desert Song," sung by the Red Shadow in *Desert Song*. I somewhat artificially came to associate the lush blue harmonies of this song—of gliding over silver-blue desert evenings on horseback—with a pretty girl named Linda who lived a block or two down our street. I did not love her or, really, know her, but she was a wonderful, teasingly potent object of my distant serenades. The instant I was let out of doors I would orient myself, as if magnetically, to Linda's house. Alert as a hawk to her sudden emergence out the door, I would delight in the golden-headed speck of her sitting on her front steps or swinging on her swings. Then, once she was fixed in my vision, I would move behind (once even inside) a bush or hedgerow where, I assumed unseen, I sang "Desert Song" with all the force I could command. It was possible, I believed, to erect a bridge of song between suburban lawn and the truer dimension of musical deserts and moonlit balconies. It was part of a dizzyingly promising process by which not Linda, but a Linda-like person, a full-grown lustrous lover, would *sing back*.

My friend Kevin Conley, whom I would meet the following year, had a real love, one who could evoke the love-feeling of the operettas. This was instructive. Her name was Brenda. Kevin would have worn gold braid for her—and in fact did wear some outlandish getups to attract her attention. He ached for her, would do dangerous things, be silly for her.

One morning he determined to wait for her, hanging by his knees, from a tree limb in her backyard, until she emerged from her back door. From my perspective as observer, the chocolate soldier-rightness of this bit of derring-do began to lose its edge the longer he hung there. As the watch grew unbearably tedious, I tried to persuade Kevin to come down and play. Brenda's house was as still as a tomb. It became impossible to imagine that anyone was at home inside, then impossible to imagine that the house had ever been inhabited. Kevin, tense and alarmingly florid, would not alter his vow.

Then noisily, spectacularly, bolts were unbolted and back door, then screen door were opened. Out into the morning light stepped Brenda. She was as bright as a lemon in yellow shorts and a white blouse.

"Hey, *Brenda!*" I hailed her.

As she spotted us and began to speak, Kevin disengaged one of his legs from the limb—hanging by one leg would be his acrobatic salute. But something went wrong—perhaps the sustained inversion had weakened him—because both legs slid over the limb, and Kevin dropped down in a heap onto the grass. He rolled over in controlled slow motion, clutching the back of his neck with one hand. He groaned. I realized at once that his pain was romantic pain. He was not hurt. Brenda ran to him and knelt over him, her exaggerated solicitude harmonizing perfectly with Kevin's halting, elaborately specific account of his injuries. Through all of it Kevin kept his eyes closed, a response I understood instinctively. To have looked up into Brenda's clean, sunburned face would have been somehow a trespass.

Brenda was fourteen, a fully developed teenager. The almost total unlikelihood of her taking him seriously as a lover seemed to free Kevin to express the very depths of his romantic feeling. He arranged his days so that he might fly past her on his bicycle at top speeds, his fingers perhaps laced casually behind his back. All street games under his

114

direction were now carried out, regardless of obstacles, directly in front of Brenda's house.

One evening when darkness had curtailed such a game, we noticed that a party or a family get-together of some kind was taking place on Brenda's screened porch. As the evening darkened we crept up close to the screens where, invisible to the guests inside the lighted enclosure, we watched the proceedings as if they were a formal entertainment. Kevin raptly followed Brenda's every gesture. When at length the party broke up and the guests had vacated the screened porch, Kevin sprang to his feet, silently opened the screen door, grabbed a tumbler from an end table, and slipped out. He raced across the darkened lawns toward his house. When I caught up with him, he was crouched at the base of his hedge, inspecting the glass.

"What did you do that for?" I asked.

"This was Brenda's glass," he said as if incanting something he had practiced. "There was iced tea in it, and Brenda drank it." This much I followed, but it seemed to lack the clarity of Kevin's other romantic gestures. Then he grew aggressive, excited.

"Brenda's *lips* were on this glass. If I put my lips in the same place—" he closed his lips over the rim of the glass— "what would be the difference," he challenged, "between that and a *kiss*?"

There would be none! I thrilled at his thrill. Kevin could keep the glass, imprinted with its glass kiss, hidden in his room and have it forever. For love's sake, I realized, love could be artfully stolen and kept. I felt undeservedly lucky, and I still do, to be a part of a world so shot through with love and with so many opportunities to steal it.

In kindergarten my love-feeling was evoked for the first time by a flesh-and-blood person: a petite, wordless fawn of a

115

girl named Gwendolyn. Her face of finely made little features was surrounded by a spectacular corona of light, frizzy hair. It was explained to the class as a body that Gwendolyn was "shy." She did not like to speak, even in reply, and we were not to bother her about it. So Gwendolyn's silence became her distinction. Gwendolyn was made for protecting, and I longed to protect her. But so gently, and yet so collectedly, did she project herself into the world, that no one thought of harming her. Voices instinctively dropped, play became orderly when Gwendolyn happened quietly onto the scene. But although there seemed to be no assignable harm from which to protect her, I decided that I would protect her generally. In what unstructured minutes of outdoor play our teacher allotted us, I would take Gwendolyn lovingly by the hand and lead her away from the other children, perhaps to a bush at the playground's edge or into the innermost cage of the jungle gym. Once I had isolated her in this way, I could not bring myself to look into her asking, glass-delicate face. Even oblique glances, the most fleeting impressions of cheek or sleeve, threatened to melt me away. So I turned my back to her and, arms crossed (I hoped) menacingly across my chest, I "guarded" her.

Not, apparently, well enough. One day she was gone from our midst, and I cannot remember an explanation. Where did she go? It is conceivable that she dissolved in a breeze. Perhaps gentleness, fragility, and silence could combine to pure ether.

Two years later love stirred me powerfully again. The fact that it did not seem to stir other second graders bothered me a little. I could accept that the love-sense of the operettas might come out of a private, narrowly accessible store, but I felt other boys, my friends, ought to be stirred by the electrifying presence of so perfect a beauty as Gail Santoro. She was more beautiful than drawings of beauties in the

116

comics. Her prettiness glittered, it *leaped out* at you as might an exceptionally striking face on the cover of a magazine. The fluffed curly blackness of her hair and her plum-dark mouth accentuated the milky smooth curves of cheek and chin. Her eyes were dark and shone like the polished black buttons embedded in the fur of the little stuffed animals created to break children's hearts.

This time I would hang on. I would open my eyes to the morning, my mind as white as the ceiling, and then I would remember. "Gail," I would say. "Gail Santoro." Then her image would appear, raven and cream. Her schoolbooks were clutched tightly to her sweater of white angora. She was laughing at me, she was murmuring like a clear brook moving over pebbles.

Gwendolyn had required protection. Gail Santoro would require declarations, significant gestures. I became an obsessive bestower of gifts. The commercial complex of the twentieth century does not produce adequate gifts of love. I needed a billowing gown of saffron brocade, inset with diamonds. I needed an ancient chest of Spanish leather, brimming over with gemstones. I needed a pearl the size of a golf ball. I pillaged through my mother's jewelry, but everything looked too dull, too heavy, too manufactured. There were so few bright *stones* in that clinking array. I took what I thought was the best of it and gave it, gravely and wordlessly, to Gail. Once with angelic tact my mother questioned me about what she must have perceived as dramatic depletions in her stock of costume jewelry. Moreover, Gail's mother had restored to her a necklace Mrs. Santoro believed might have been valuable. I found the subject impossible to discuss. "I was just playing a game," I lied impatiently.

One afternoon while out investigating a thicket in the fields, I became distracted by great clusters of velvety maroon ornaments suspended just overhead: the flowers or

117

fruits of the purple sumac trees growing in profusion. I plucked one from its stem and ran my fingers over its deep-red nap. This was beautiful. It belonged to the plush, liveried era of chocolate soldiers, elegant coaches, and swordplay. I gathered all the sumac fruits I could hold. These, I felt, were durable. These would be suitable gifts for Gail Santoro.

When the following day I upended a shopping bag full of them on her desk, they were received with delighted bewilderment. The other girls standing around went into a little frenzy of nervous laughter. "*Somebody's* got a girlfriend." "Somebody's in love with Gail!" Girls, I thought. I could stand the charges.

I cannot remember a single moment alone with Gail Santoro, nor do I recall a specific word spoken between us. She was always flanked by two or three friends, friends who made all the noise, who provided all the words. Gail was always turning to go, to go to lunch, to go back to class, to go home. She took me in with her eyes, she laughed at what I said, she was openly, even cheerfully, aware of me. But there was no sign whatsoever that she needed me, that she awoke to first light and said my name.

In time, due to the sheer distance she kept, Gail Santoro "wore off." I continued to know her throughout my childhood, but I could not stir up any feeling for her, beyond what courtesy occasionally required. Though, literally, a "beautiful doll" even unto young womanhood, she seemed to turn no heads. My gift of sumac may have been the only one strewn in her path.

Many years later, in England, working in a deserted alcove of the Cambridge University library, I was transported so vividly and powerfully back into my tenth year that, emotionally, I was there again. This was a revisitation, no mere "memory." I was stupefied. A moment earlier the library windows had been streaked with rain. Beyond, the gray, swollen sky was as close as fur. Then the library ceiling, the sky itself, opened up into the clear blue light of an Illinois afternoon. Down out of that cool sky I dropped into a great mound of straw. It was straw from a construction site at the edge of the fields. Next to me, blond hair tousled about her ruddy cheeks, was a girl wearing a look of unrestrained hilarity. It was a girl with the miraculous name of Tricia Treat. We had just jumped together into the straw from a bulldozed bluff of earth.

Tricia Treat was the first girl to sing back to me. How had I possibly forgotten her? How could I have forgotten her *completely?* We scrambled out of the straw and ran up the hill to leap again. I wanted to leap into the blue air with Tricia Treat, to fly with her, until the sky went dark. And then, in a wave of unspeakable pleasure, I realized I had done it.

The love of Tricia Treat was introduced to me in the fifth grade on the first day of school. I was sitting at my desk not fully awake, not yet emerged out of glimmering summer. An enormous blond girl, a cheerful Swede twice my size named Katie Nygaard, leaned over my desk and said, "Do you know Tricia Treat?" I did not, but the name! "Did you know Tricia Treat *likes* you?" Katie asked, grinning crazily. I didn't know. The news was uncomfortably personal. I twisted in my chair to locate somebody who looked like the name Tricia Treat. "*There* she is," said Katie Nygaard the instant I spotted Tricia. There she was. A bird's nest tousle of straw-colored hair over a sunburned face. No indirection, no distance—this was no silent Gwendolyn, no Gail Santoro. Tricia Treat—toothsome and glad, eyes full of plans—returned my look with an expansive grin. Everything about her was saying, as puppies say when you enter a room, "Hello!" Everything about her was asking, "What are you *like?"* She was an infinitely appealing invitation to play. "Tell her," I said to the imposing Katie Nygaard, "I like her, too."

For almost a year I dwelled with Tricia Treat in the center of a garden of Play. During unmonitored hours, in school and out, we were inseparable. There were thousands of unmonitored hours, often ten in a day. How was this possible? Perhaps the love of ten-year-olds confers with it invisibility. Perhaps its onset is so quick and so startling to adults that, like hummingbirds on Wall Street, it is screened out of vision. Perhaps we simply outran all attempts to keep track of us. Every boy and girl in the school paired our names. We were not two things paired; we were one thing, double-named. We were so sure of each other that we were never exclusive, almost never alone. We were happy and so full of ecstatic prospects that an enthusiastic company of my friends and a similar company of Tricia's friends joined our union. We peopled every imaginable posse, staffed dozens of construction projects, were ample for two sides of any game or sport. If we separated sometimes by gender, it was only to heighten the satisfaction of reuniting. The governing idea was to apply special inventiveness in order to raise the company to the highest possible pitch of elation, then to hold onto it in celebration. Tricia and I were consulted in all things, proposed the games, made up the rules. Our deliberations consisted of, "What if——?" Our commands were, "Let's play——," "Let's try——," "Let's go——." By virtue of the superior purity of our childishness, and perhaps due to some perceived quality in our affection, we were cast as Parents—as child-parents.

We heard the mayor's wife was dying, so we trooped over to his lawn and sang camp songs, we believed consolingly.

A rabid dog had been reported on the north side of the

tracks. We combed the north side en masse, thrilled to be risking a deadly attack.

A genuine bully, an older boy named Terrence Van Zandt, with a nose that hooked down almost to his upper lip, had set up camp on the playground after school. We marched to him, as to war, even in some kind of file, to suggest a crusade. When, shrill and inarticulate, we approached him, we were astounded to find that there was no strength in our numbers. Each of us was thrown off, slapped, chased, his or her arm twisted at Terrence Van Zandt's pleasure.

Clearly it was up to me, Tricia at my side. Tricia swelled in hatred of Terrence Van Zandt. I hailed him, addressing him coarsely by his last name.

"Why don't you stop beating up little kids?" I shouted.

He swaggered up to within an inch of my face.

"What did you say?"

"Why don't you stop beating up little kids?"

Terrence Van Zandt picked me up at the legs, slung me over his shoulders, spun me around until he himself was dizzy, then threw me down into a sandbox.

"You stink," said Tricia, fearless, to the unmoved Terrence.

I got up out of the sand. "Afraid to pick on somebody your own size?"

He tried to slap my face—a humiliation I would not endure. When I shielded myself, Terrence Van Zandt, thrusting one leg behind me, pushed me down over it into the dirt. Banged up, arms akimbo (again), a little short of breath, it occurred to me that I could endure these blows indefinitely.

I heard Tricia say, "You still stink."

On my feet again, I repeated, "Afraid to pick on somebody your own size?" He knocked me down again, this time very quickly.

Just as quickly I was back on my feet. The excitement of the confrontation had diminished sharply. Our friends formed a nagging, perhaps even slightly bored crescent around Terrence, Tricia, and me.

"So you can knock me down—*big deal,*" I said. I was determined to be invincible in my openness to attack.

"I'm going to break your arm," said Terrence evenly.

He spun me around by the shoulders, grabbed my wrist, and pulled it up high between my shoulder blades. There was a flash of yellow pain. I screamed.

"Oh," said Tricia in withering disgust, "do you ever stink," and she kicked Terrence's backside. As I whimpered with the searing hurt, Terrence became confused. He had not dispersed us or frightened the group by tossing me here and there. He had me, he was hurting me, and I was clearly crying. Why didn't I give up? Plead for something? An aggravating weight seemed to fall on all of us. It said: "This isn't terror, this isn't even a fight—it's just an older boy hurting a younger one." The situation was making us, including Terrence, tired. The taunts from the crescent—"you stink," "you jerk"—were losing force. Even I saw clearly that it would do Terrence no good to break my arm, so I said, between gasps, "Break my arm, I don't care."

Terrence released his hold, threw me down again, and walked off, to a chorus of hooting disparagement. Two or three times he wheeled around and lofted a stone in our direction. At last he turned a corner and disappeared.

Victory! And only I could have done it. That answer, every answer, was so clear, so easy. You just *presented* yourself in any situation, and there would be a prize, a victory, some surprising pleasure. And each one was real because it was shared. Tricia never executed a dive, never got off a joke that was not my triumph also.

I became aware that there was a book Tricia and her

friends were reading. It elicited excited, cryptic talk. What's it about, I demanded of Katie Nygaard, the giantess. "It's about us!" she burst out loonily, "about kids exactly like us, and it's all about this little *French* boy . . ." Katie was crazy, so I would have to read it for myself. The book was called *Best Friends,* and I was the first boy in town to have checked it out of the library. As usual, Katie was exactly right. It was about us—not us specifically—but about children held fast in their love of one another. The children were charged with the same self-affirming delight we knew. The children themselves nearly named the feeling (love), but the sacred word, although instinctively understood, was inutterable. "Friendship," understood in a new way, through literature, would suffice. I was awed and deeply reassured that the writers of books understood the love-feeling of children and were willing to put it up for show.

The clear purpose of every day was to revitalize the quality of best-friendship. And, generously, it was always revitalized at the first sight of Tricia in the morning. At a point in late evening, starlight would descend to earth in the flickering of fireflies, and there was everywhere the promise of Tricia curled up, hiding at the bottom of the hedge, or the luminescent presence of her white blouse at my side as we glided over lawns, chased or on the chase. Our best-friendship sometimes raised its pitch to a point of tingling. At that point we might glide silently off to a lawn apart, a lawn the texture of carpet, the color of smoke, and might stand back-to-back, skull-to-skull, craning out necks to take in all the stars there were. At that pitch neither of us could speak a word.

It is hard to imagine now what we did with so much feeling. But of course we moved with it; driven by it, we ran. I have a persistant image of Tricia: she is waiting for me to catch up to her, perhaps to be let out of school or out of the house. She is stationary but not still. She seems somehow to be idling like a car. As I approach she half turns to me, absently slapping a leg as if lashing a metaphysical horse, until I am at her side—in the metaphysical saddle—and we are off. Being with Tricia meant *moving* with her, at her side, in front of her, to fetch or find her, at best moving with her at nightfall, amid a pack of friends anonymous as extra selves.

No trace of intelligent restraint shaped or bounded our play. The dynamics of "what if——?" and "Let's try——" sent us all over town, at all hours. In the spring of that school year it frequently sent us, odd to recall, to the town luncheonette instead of to the school cafeteria. It was Tricia's idea. She had dined there often enough with her family and had acquired a taste for some of its short-order specialties. What if we all went, without the slowing, inhibiting presence of an adult? School children were allowed to carry their lunches to school or to purchase them in the cafeteria, but everybody was required to eat there. Eating in the cafeteria was as fundamental as school itself.

It was a perfect idea: daring, impossible, unprecedented. Once slyly past the imaginary sentries of the playground, we headed off—many times, as it turned out—in a pack of six or seven. Where did we get the money? Who knows? Adventurers find a way. Racing, chasing, roughhousing along the budding, blooming lawns, we disturbed the peace, both going and coming. Tables had to be joined, extra places set for us. Nothing is more screamingly funny to a ten-year-old, particularly if flamboyantly truant, than to order lunch from a menu, then to try to eat it decorously among the bankers, bakers, and real estate agents of one's town. Maintaining composure was a test we failed repeatedly. Tricia sat up tall, radiant in the midst of so much blurt and spray.

Sometimes Tricia and I would go to the luncheonette

alone, and these were, by contrast, still and dreamy outings. Practiced diners now, we would order without meeting the waitress's eye. We said little, even grew sleepy watching the sun-blanched commerce beyond the luncheonette window. The staff would be closing up all around us, the luncheon crowd long gone when Tricia and I rose to go. Because the school lunch break was forty-five minutes, including play, we must have been phenomenally late.

By the time the commencement of true summer caused us to be separated and shunted off willy-nilly to camps, to grandparents, and to cabins in the north woods, it had occurred to Tricia and me that just across the street from the luncheonette was the train station. What was at first a barely conceivable "what if——?"—luncheon in Chicago—was fast becoming an alluring "let's go——." I like to think that there is a detached child-part of me there now, with Tricia, seated close to the window of a coffee shop along the bottom of one of Chicago's deep, teeming canyons. Or perhaps we are walking, our arms brushing with each stride, across sparkling Michigan Avenue toward the deep blue rim of the lake, unrelenting wind full in our faces. Tricia turns to me, slaps her leg expectantly, and we run.

There was no reunion at summer's end. There was no recurrence, I am sure, of the unity and of the unearthly vibrancy of the past year's best-friendships. I wonder what factor in development, what warp in memory, what failure of allegiance accounts for the termination of such enchantment. I know that Tricia Treat did not move away because I remember her, imperfectly, as a pleasant, smiling presence around the periphery of my later adolescence. I am sure I could find her picture in my high school yearbook.

If I consider them all together—the chocolate soldier's

lady, Gwendolyn, Gail Santoro, Tricia Treat—not analyzing them but just letting their recollected essences arrange themselves in my consciousness, they come to resemble a configuration of angels. Each of them, in sequence, pierced me with the love-sense. And although each individual experience is wonderfully distinctive, each was an instance of the same great thing. They were, I believe, angels of love.

These early angels, it is clear now, were forerunners. I would soon know another kind of love, a love that contains all particular loves, as a world contains all of its creatures. But meeting this new love, as I did, in a lovely person, I was confused. I wanted to unite with her in love, as I had united with Tricia in play. I wanted to engage Love itself for my exclusive delight.

It was terrible to learn that Love encompasses infinitely more than the traces of beauty and the teasing sweetnesses I had been able to perceive as a child. I had not yet faced the exquisite, self-annihilating pain that follows any encounter with Love itself (nor in the event was I graceful in response). The mystery that love lost is the beginning, not the end, of one's mature story took me twenty years even to begin to grasp. Although some of the mystery was hinted at by the angels, its full expression required the presence of Diana West.

In even the longest, most elaborate life stories, only two or three things happen: love, the slow awakening to one's work, and death. The spirit is alive to these things, and only to these things. Rising to them is all the life there is. Integrating them into ourselves takes up all our time. Love in its fullest expression happened to me (it is still happening) when I beheld Diana West and then, as if I had been impatiently waiting for twelve years to do it, gave myself away to her entirely.

Diana West is not an exaggerated infatuation, not

merely the target of dammed-up adolescent libido. (Of course she was, but that is not even the doorstep to the rest of what she was.) People in all walks of life knew exactly what Diana West was, although there were not always the words for it. Her own mother and father instinctively gave her the distance and the reverent regard that, in my imagination, Joseph and Mary gave to Jesus. Mr. Giroux, a ravaged Elijah-like character whose eyes burned and bulged beneath his glasses when he spoke, whose bony, beaky presence was the demon-genius of our junior high school, taught Diana and seemed to know all about her. Once, four years after I had had Diana and lost her, he stopped me in a supermarket parking lot, desperate to tell me something. Knowing somehow that no polite preamble would be necessary to acknowledge the four-year hiatus in our own acquaintance, Mr. Giroux tapped a finger into the center of my chest. "You are not going to forget that girl," he said. "You are going to love her forever." His words, because they were true and because I had been denying them, burned through my chest like a brand. Another teacher, my high school drama coach, was musing about Diana in my presence once; I was so desperate to hear his appraisal, I did not let on that I knew her (that I held the idea of her in my innards like the stolen core of the sun). "Diane West," he said thoughtfully, "does not seem to be anything like a teenager. She seems to be a lady."

She was a lady. She was not "old for her age"—in either appearance or behavior. Although substantially a woman by the time I met her at twelve, she was really no assignable age; she was lady-age.

In junior high school childhood was over. As if to acknowledge this, the town school system streamed youth together from all of its scattered primary schools. In this exciting, important blending of tribes, one scouted, in the company of perhaps one or two friends, for a new place.

Mental quickness mattered now; graded work now transformed what had been the natural aura of "smart kids" and "dumb kids" into precise public realities. The spontaneity of games was over. One now would have to compete, against strangers, to wear the school colors in sports. One would, or would not, make a place here. There was no life worth having outside of this school. In the physical power and beauty of its broad-shouldered older boys and its long-legged girls lay, at last, a credible, desirable future.

Everybody was new, and so everybody needed to be pointed out. "That's Diana West," said the boy seated directly across the cafeteria table. He pointed over my head. I twisted around reflexively and scanned the brilliantly sunlit aisle formed between our row of tables and the wall of cafeteria windows. Proceeding past me through this white light was a pair of girls in animated conversation. One was a blur; the other seemed to proceed through the visual pathways into the center of my brain where, displacing whatever had been there, her image flashed like a single frame of bright film. At the moment of this possession, Diana's friend is in the process of relating some incident, apparently funny. Diana's dark eyes are slightly averted in attention. Her lips are parted, and she is forming a smile in anticipation of a laugh. Although there is no trace of hilarity, her smile is wonderfully generous. It has already accepted the story and its teller. It is a smile in love with all stories told for delight. A smile on the brink of laughter is the loveliest expression of the human face.

Time resumed. Diana West and her companion passed by. She was going to be president of the student council, somebody said. I could not have cared less. Something so stirring, so important was happening to me that I had to struggle to figure out the first thing to do about it. I had to find her. I could not possess her, I could not hold her still long enough even to sort out what was happening to me until I first found her. What had she looked like? Her face and the white light from the windows were becoming interchangeable. Then, finally there was an impression of the slightly sharp angle of her chin, something of the same angle—something—in the *v* of her smile, something of it again in the chiseled lines of her nose. Her eyes were dark—holding the glint of something on the brink of expression. Framing her face were waves of deep brown hair, hair of every color from honey to scarlet to black. There was something angular and acute about her: high, delicate cheekbones, again the chin, shins, wrists, ankles, long slender fingers. There was a fleeting impression of a collie. An impression of a doe. There were hundreds of noisy boys and girls milling about the cafeteria. Where was she?

Against one wall of the cafeteria a long line had formed waiting to purchase the student council's candy. At its midpoint, arresting as a delicate thoroughbred in a close procession of automobiles, stood Diana West, still listening attentively to her friend. Without deliberation I insinuated myself up close to the candy table, then by imperceptible half steps and nudges, moved around behind it, where, saying nothing and absently rearranging the bars of candy on display, I appeared to be one of the student vendors. I answered a few questions about price.

Then Diana and her friend were standing across the table. Something lighthearted was being said about the selection. As Diana looked up to declare her purchase, smiling as if in anticipation of some universally acknowledged good, I spoke up very loudly.

"Nothing here for under a hundred dollars."

There was a noisy response to this generally, but my eyes were fixed on Diana West's. Her smile froze, then thawed, then widened. With a wideness of eye appropriate to acknowledging, generously, a surprising statement, she registered no surprise whatsoever. Her smile in response to me—were we looking at one another for twenty minutes?—said: "To think that you have made a joke for no other reason that to delight me. How *glad* that makes me—how glad for you and for jokes."

Diana West was the most finished, the most perfectly intact person I have ever met. She spoke openly and well, but she was not effusive, especially in groups. (This should have been more instructive for me than it was.) She seemed in all situations paranormally alert to nuance, actively working to take in everything taking place and every word that was said. Without apparent effort, she charmed people of all ages by paying intensely close attention to everything they said.

She laughed often and easily, but was never hysterical or silly, even among her friends who so often were. She liked genuine oddity. She also followed with special delight any account of great effort coming to nothing. Well-intentioned non sequiturs came closest to undoing her. With Diana there was never any question of coarseness or cruelty. Not only was it unthinkable that she would initiate anything coarse or cruel herself, but also her presence discouraged vulgarity and meanness to a remarkable extent. In all relationships, in all groups, a tacit and decidedly agreeable rule prevailed: Diana is good; we must be good likewise.

Although the question never occurred to me at the time, I wonder now what any of us meant to her. She seemed full of affection for, and interest in, everybody, and although physically always closely attached, she could not really be said to *need* anybody. To me especially, a burning ambition on her part, a stated need, an obsession would have been welcome—I would happily have made a grail out of any desire of Diana's. But such desires were impossible to iden-

130

tify, and the longer I knew Diana, the more troubling this became for me. Considered objectively, Diana's contribution to others, individually and in groups, was to acknowledge what *we* cared about, what we were. I have already mentioned her gift of acknowledging humor. Again it was not the jokes themselves that surprised her and made her laugh (with the exception of a certain kind of failed, mistold joke), but she seemed genuinely moved by anyone taking pains to create humor. Diana West did not create "fun," but she *confirmed* it and in so doing celebrated the best in us. She also—and this may have been her most cherished quality— acknowledged our innermost plans. Everyone I knew well, boy or girl, became an unself-conscious confessor of personal dreams and desires to Diana. Her solicitude and deep interest transformed hopes into convictions.

But she could not have this gift for confirming others' experiences without corresponding empathy for their disappointments, hurts, and losses. Diana herself had no defenses against being hurt, which is why it was unthinkable to try to hurt her (although, as I will explain, I made some desperate attempts at it later). She was open to everybody else's pain. What did she do with it? I do not ever remember seeing her cry, nor did I ever see her rebuke anybody, nor, not even once, to complain about anything. Yet I know she took in everything, felt everything, and what was painful hurt her.

I became convinced of the acute pitch of her sensitivity one evening at a small party. Perhaps a dozen of us were seated on or standing about a cluster of outdoor furniture in somebody's backyard. The 45 r.p.m. hits of the day were being played on a portable record player on a picnic table. Three or four boys, including me, were discussing the merits of the "hits." Into a lapse in our discussion came the opening phrases of a song we had just evaluated and dismissed. Too loudly I sang out, "Who's the *jerk* who's playing this?" The

131

instant I spoke the word "jerk," with its extra emphasis, I spotted Diana in my peripheral vision. She started—a shudder of head, neck, and shoulders—as if a sharp bang had been detonated nearby or as if she had suddenly been reminded of something intolerable. I saw her only in profile, and although she clearly knew that I had just spoken, she did not turn to look at me. The eye I could see had closed tightly at the hurtful word, then opened without seeing. Her mouth fell slack. Barely perceptibly, she nodded her head, a gesture somehow equivalent to swallowing something with difficulty. She was swallowing my unfeeling thoughtlessness. *No one ought to feel a "jerk" for playing a tune he or she likes.* For playing any tune. Perhaps *Diana had wanted to hear it.* It would be worse, I knew, if it had been somebody else. *Jerk*—the word, sharply as I had said it, swirled around my head, rang out over the town. Because Diana had felt it, my unkindness was real. It was not one of the thousands of other things that I did; it was a distinct thing unto itself, a sharp-edged thing that stabbed like a knife.

Because Diana West registered everything that was true in the people she knew, now including me, she would of course register my love. My love was so completely unqualified and so urgent that for a long time it left me as vulnerable as she was. Knowing this—I think it was knowing this—she did two soaringly generous things (or are they one?) in response: she let me love her, and she loved me back. But it would take some time before I realized that she could not love me in the same way I loved her.

After my vision of her in the cafeteria, I managed to be whenever possible either right behind her or, unexpectedly (I hoped), right in front of her. I learned where she lived (far across town), located her locker, learned which rooms she occupied, with which students and with which teachers. It was essential that I engage her attention. I told jokes, made cracks whenever I was in her range of hearing. Next best, I reasoned, was to puzzle her; love *might* begin with wonderment. She would have to think something, and to think it in connection with me, if I presented her with thirty cartons of milk at her lunch table, if, recklessly truant, I walked by the open door of *all* of her classes carrying a placard of greeting. Student suitors of that period carried the books of their intendeds; I asked Diana if she would like to carry mine. But I carried hers, giving them up at the classroom door with a reluctance that was less a joke than she may have imagined.

Then one day a disclosure was made to me that opened me to a dimension of ecstasy until then unknown. After lunch one of Diana's friends was waiting at my locker. She looked dazed, almost sleepy with stupefaction.

"Guess who likes you?" she asked.

"Who likes me?"

"Guess."

"Who likes me?"

"Oh, somebody who just spent a whole period writing your name."

"Oh, sure."

"Want to see?"

The girl unfolded a piece of notebook paper, covered with Diana's delicate, vertical script. I grabbed for it, and the friend ran away. I chased her, caught her, pried the paper out of the hand of the hysterically giggling girl.

There it was. My name (or a diminutive form of it: Ricky) closely written perhaps four hundred times on the front and back of a sheet of notebook paper. I took it with me to class, read it, and reread it all afternoon. RICKY RICKY RICKY RICKY—four hundred times. The last line read RICKY RICKY RICKY—OH RICKY!

After school I spotted her in the corridor traffic and stepped into her path. She smiled beautifully and put the

133

heel of her hand to her forehead in a gesture of exaggerated chagrin.

"Sally gave—" she said. "I'm so embarrassed."

She did not look embarrassed. She looked glad.

Only late that night, too happy, too agitated to sleep, did I put the event in perspective. *She had written my name.* Diana had acted on me, had voluntarily inscribed me. I was substantial. I was come to life. I was all over the page. OH RICKY!

With love acknowledged comes the initiation into love's ancient rites. The first of these is the dance. The junior high school offered a program of Noon Dancing between lunchtime and afternoon classes. An alternative to outdoor play, it was perhaps conceived—who knows—as an aid to digestion. Whatever the intent, we were allowed to escape the gleaming momentum of school into the coolness of the massively vaulted old gymnasium. There in a light like butterscotch, we moved over the maple-colored floor in the figures of the dance. The music was the popular ballads of the day, the records amplified to a fullness it seemed possible to enter. (To think that it was true. Noon Dancing has since been dropped from the junior high school program, and I am sure from every junior high school in the world.) What a blessing—to have been provided by the authorities that half-lit pocket of romantic time. The *words* of those ballads—was the student council, its advisor, anybody in charge *aware* of what was being unloosed?

> Heavenly shades of night are falling,
> It's twilight time.
> Out of the mist your voice is calling,
> It's twilight time.

And

> My prayer—is to linger with you
> Till the end of the day
> For as long as I live . . .

Most dances were announced as Men's Choices, but there were also Ladies' Choices, Free Choices (in which boys or girls could seek partners of either gender). There were also group dances like the Bunny Hop and the Stroll, and Progressives, in which a single couple would dance until instructed to change partners and so on, until the floor was filled. The figures of the dance.

We were not allowed to run, so when the voice over the microphone said, "Men's Choice," I would execute a very unusual straight-legged shuffle, the forward angle of my body seeming to defy gravity. By the time the other boys had begun to cross the floor, I was already reaching for Diana's hand. I never considered another partner, and when Ladies' Choices were called, she would choose me, although she did not hurry across the floor. I don't believe I was ever confident that she would come. However many hundreds of times I asked Diana to dance, it fascinated me that she always took care to *accept* the invitation. There was a perceptible instant in which she took in who I was (and possibly, humiliating to consider, what I was), that I was making an offer of some kind—to dance—and that this offer was a rival claim to every other possibility of the moment. And *yes,* what a pleasure it would be for her to dance with me again.

The fast dances were obligations. The slow ones, fox trots and waltzes, were ancient and sacred. It might have occurred to someone, to an adult, watching us (watching me in particular), that early adolescents are awkward dancers: all elbows and stiffness. We seemed less to hold our partners in a meandering embrace than to be pushing them Germanically away from us. There appeared to be something clumping and obligatory about the way we stepped through our prescribed patterns.

But the visual evidence of us in the gym did not tell the story. Our stiffness was not aversion. It was certainly not a lack of coordination. No one moves with more instinctive fluidity to music than an adolescent does. I held Diana apart from me, monitoring a finely gauged level of resistance to her, in order to maintain consciousness. Moving with her, just inches separating us, my jaw locked, neck held so that I looked past her cheek, past the rim of her ear, past wisps of her hair, an irresistible current pulsed through me; only at a remove was it possible to breathe. Sometimes my resistance failed, and I lost control. This was typically when I had let myself ascend into the imagery of the ballads, where "heavenly shades of night were falling." More than once did I awake, to loathesome teasing, to find that we were dancing after the music had stopped. (What deep courtesy on Diana's part to have continued with me.) Each direct point of contact—the joining of our hands, my palm around the curve of her waist, hers upon my shoulder—conducted a special current of its own. The current was nearly unbearable where palm met palm, although by holding the clasp perfectly still throughout the dance, I was able to produce some slight anesthesia. It was very simple. Joined together in the dance, knowing what I knew (OH RICKY!), feeling what I felt, Diana was formally mine. All other feeling was either anticipation or afterglow of our communion in dance.

Only once or twice later on, and then at an evening party, did we close the distance of the dance (did *I* close it?), so that Diana's wispy temple touched my cheek, and her bosom just met my chest. I closed my eyes and gave up. I was aware of some scent on her vulnerable neck. Seeing nothing, I let myself be lost in the impression of Diana as sheer matter. Holding her lightly to me, our heads touching, I felt myself moving through, melding without resistance into her body. Her fingers moved over mine, and the currents splayed through me liked charged flashes of light.

I passed over some kind of barrier. Now whenever I was home, outside shooting baskets, inside playing the piano, the currents ran. I felt afloat, adrift with no possible footing. I had to have more of Diana—no, I had to have all of Diana. But even as it drove me on, I knew this very desire was going to spoil everything. There was no form, no imaginable dance to contain it. I did not, primarily, want more of her physically; I wanted the state of being, the core of grace that made touching her hand the experience it was.

A wealthy classmate of mine, a tidy, childlike boy who lived behind pillars in the town's stateliest house, invited a dozen of us, including Diana and me, to a party that would conclude in a hayride. The night of the party we were taxied to a rural stable where a glassy frost had already stiffened the grasses underfoot. It was early November, wonderfully cold and clear. A nearly full moon glowed overhead, close to earth. The exhalations of our breath hung before us in illuminated puffs. The wagon was small, and we had to bunch together tightly to fit inside, a jumble of heavy coats and sweaters in the straw. There was exhilarated talk and laughter at first, but then we were quieted by the almost musical clopping of the horses' hooves over the cold wagon path, the good musk smell of the straw, the dreamy expanses of moon-blanched cornfields on either side, then the enclosing walls of a wood, the white moon weaving in and out of the open cut of sky overhead. The ride was very long, but from

137

the moment it began, I wanted it never to end. Diana and I sat shoulder to shoulder, almost reclining against the side of the wagon. I could see knees of the others, sleeves, a bob of hair, and straw, but no whole person. I turned to look at Diana, and at that moment she turned to look at me. I could look only for a second. Inside my chest I felt as if overtaut strings were being strummed repeatedly, and nothing I could do would stop the swelling resonance. Soundlessly, without tears, and out of an ancient sense of beauty, I cried. Then I initiated my first deliberate act of physical lovemaking. I eased my arm over Diana's head and placed it down over her shoulder and, without looking at her, pulled her gently closer. She half turned to me, then nestled down along my side, her head resting against my collar. All that moved was the wagon. All that sounded were the wheels and the horses' hooves. I looked up at the moon, and without words or ideas, prayed. There was a preverbal gratitude, and there was a terrible longing for something which, I would intermittently realize, I held securely at my side. I know I prayed that the hayride would continue forever, but it ended that night.

I have said already that I knew, even before the hayride, that there was no imaginable condition I could bring about—no form—that could contain the love I felt for Diana West. The profoundest condition I knew about was marriage, which was not only practically unthinkable, but also it was not what I wanted for Diana. I could imagine us together in flight; I could imagine running away with her through fantastic networks of trains, tunnels, and streets of distant cities. But Diana would never run off; she so abundantly belonged where she was. I had to do something. I was becoming irascible, reckless. For reasons I did not understand myself, I tried to provoke Diana into making dramatic responses to me.

One day I decided not to speak to her or to look at her.

At Noon Dancing I sat blank-faced on the boys'-side bench. Finally there was a Ladies' Choice, and through a forest of adolescents she made her way to me, tentative and inquiring as a deer. I got up to dance, my pulse pounding audibly in my skull, and I neither answered her questions ("Is something the matter?" "Are you mad at me?"), nor looked at her as we danced. Later, angrily, I dismissed the inquiries of her friends. Afterward, I was unhappy, furious with myself. I seemed bent on becoming vile, also unable to stop myself. I was motivated by the unexamined principle that, because I could not exclusively and forever possess Diana West in love, then the hell of the alternative might just as well begin.

But to the extent it did begin, I felt a terror I could not bear, a premonition of a loss so massive I believed I could disappear into it. Because I could not really understand Diana, I would lose her. What I did not understand, I see now, was the very thing I loved: her goodness. Beauty, panache, talent—for these qualities I felt I had a special sense, but before Goodness I stood as uncomprehending as a chimpanzee. I did not know that a soul like Diana West's absorbed hurts and losses like a sponge. By bearing a slight, such as my impulsive refusal to speak, she grew softer, wiser, more lovingly regardful than ever. I did not understand how she grew better as I grew worse, but I did feel my love grow more desperate with every increment of new distance between us. Helpless and miserable, I was teaching her (the truth) that investing feeling in me would be risky and occasionally hurtful.

There was no earthly end to what I wanted. I am sure that the instant I first attempted to manipulate Diana West's feelings, she began to adjust to getting along without me. The intuition of this development alternately intensified my need to show Diana the extent of my love and my desire to spoil it altogether. In the process of this destructive ambivalence, I lost my confidence, lost the spontaneous grace a lover needs to be loved in return.

In the panic of falling helplessly away from Diana West, I determined to reinstate myself by willed gestures. Seeking to bind her to me, I put together all the money I could get hold of and one winter day raced into town during the school lunch period to purchase a ring at the jewelry store. I had in mind a plain beveled band of silver or gold: something substantial and permanent. The jeweler had nothing like that. He told me I was probably thinking of a "friendship ring." He showed me a silver ring, embossed all around its circumference with little hearts. I wasn't sure about it. It was shinier than the silver I imagined. The jeweler assured me that "friendship rings" were what the high school boys gave their girls when they decided to "go steady." In my characteristic frame of mind at the time, I accepted what he said as true and bought the ring, although neither believing what he said nor liking the ring at all.

I managed to get back to school in time for the end of Noon Dancing. There was one more Men's Choice, a fast dance, and I danced it with Diana, saying very little. The bell rang, she thanked me, and turned to gather her books for class. I grabbed her hand and pulled her back to me. "This is for you," I said, and pressed the small box into her hand. She opened it, considered the ring, then made a little groan.

"Look what you've done," she said. She seemed upset, also moved. Then she took *my* hand, squeezed it, and went off.

Although miserably tense by the end of the school day, I was not really surprised when Diana's friend Sally met me at my locker after school. With a gravity that foretold everything, she handed me the jeweler's box. "Diana asked me to give this to you," she said. "There's a note inside."

When I was alone, I opened the box and read the lovely script.

This is the most special gift anyone has ever given to me. I have to return it because it is too much. Please understand. Bless you.

Love, Diana

Whereas I had been aware of a sickening, sliding sensation for days, now I was falling—OH RICKY!—and there was no way back.

I managed to prolong the falling with many more willed gestures. Each was conceived and executed in hopelessness. In the spring of that year—the worst imaginable season for regaining lost love—I took to insisting that Diana let me walk her home. I insisted, each time, that there was something I had to explain. She lived at the far edge of the north side of town, far enough away to qualify to ride the bus. It was over an hour's walk, and the way I arranged it, it might take two hours. Carrying Diana's books, I could determine the pace; there was much gloomy stopping and sitting dejectedly on the curb.

Soon after the offering of the ring, I became relegated to the station of "friend." I had given her a five-and-dime diary filled completely with desperate declarations of feeling (written in the course of a single long night), and she wrote back that she hoped I could care for her as a friend, as I would always be a "special friend" to her. To this she added, already worlds away from me, "I will never forget you." The agenda—but it was only a dream agenda—of the after-school forced marches to which Diana submitted with such graceful resignation was always the same: to restore her to my heart. Sometimes I could not find words even to approach the subject; these were the longest walks. Even when

141

I did, with tortured indirection, express something of my desire, it was after a soliloquy of perhaps an hour in which every subject, every person touched upon was angrily or superciliously dismissed. Falling and falling. Sometimes I would affect (I believe I affected) lunacy. I would say the first thing that came to mind, provided it was startling. I made terrible declarations: "Today I wanted to kill everybody in the gym," "I am going to wear these clothes I have on until I die," "Every person in my family has tuberculosis," "Come with me to Denver." Just noise, part of the sound of falling. I was tiresome.

I was also cruel, first outside of Diana's presence, then directly to her. I recall being particularly murderous to a benign, thick-featured boy named Joel Gregg. Joel Gregg had been a valued friend before Diana and he would be again after junior high school. Picking up some subconscious signal, he sensed something exciting in the drama of my quest to regain Diana West. Joel Gregg was nothing but friendly. Onto his great square head—I always think of a television screen—were placed, as if hastily, crude round features. His nose was bunched into the center of the screen like a little mound of dough. Similar pats of dough were stuck onto the sides of his head for ears. His lips were so full they appeared always to be painfully swollen. The most distinctive of his features, his lips seemed to lag behind the other movements of his mouth when he spoke, so there was a sloppy, babylike quality to his speech.

Because adolescent boys express affection through ritualistic competition, Joel got hold of the idea that he would compete with me for Diana's favor. With another girl, at another time, I would have seen in Joel's gesture the gentle tribute that it was. Joel Gregg did not, I am sure, *want* Diana West; I think he wanted to touch, just to touch, what he perceived to be remarkable feeling in my pursuit of her. In the spirit of a close friend inviting another to box, he wanted to make contact with me.

Nevertheless, Joel Gregg, whose desk abutted mine in several classes, wrote notes to Diana West, and the notes were answered. Even a glimpse of the familiar, engraved-looking script above his shirt pocket closed my stomach like a fist. He delightedly mistook my agitation and sharp words for an enthusiastic assumption of my role in the game-competition. "Whatsa matter?" he said thickly, eyes flashing in fun. "*Jealous?*"

"Of a fat, stupid dip like you?" I said, wanting to part the flesh of his throat with my hands, wanting to grind my teeth into the doughy flesh of his face.

Joel escalated the competition. He began telephoning Diana, the next day recounting for me the length of the calls. By the very nature of the game he found himself being pulled adoringly toward Diana—a bonus that delighted him. He began to glow with an unconcealed happiness I wanted to poison. He told me he had arranged to walk her home. This I refused to believe; "Oh, *that* I'd like to see."

"Watch us," he smiled, pleased as Buddha.

I did watch, poised like a burglar behind the glass of the school doors. I watched them head northward together in the gauzy spring light. I watched them until they disappeared.

Joel thought I was playing my part with extravagant flamboyance. I knew I was only with effort containing a volcanic rage. When he paused at my locker to announce that he thought he would ask Diana to an approaching school dance (the only dance the school held), resistance failed. For a moment I could not see anything at all. Then I saw Joel Gregg smiling, standing much too close to me.

"*Move*—you stupid fat-lipped bag of pus!"

Hoping to shatter him like glass, I punched him full on the mouth, splitting his too-full lips against his teeth. Blood

143

filled the spaces between his teeth and ran over his lips onto his chin. His eyes enlarged with tears. After that I can remember only flailing and clinching, strangled oaths, the salt of blood and tears on my tongue. I was sent home. Falling, falling.

I had to stay away from people now. (I was ordered to, but the orders were unnecessary.) I was supposed to stay away from Joel Gregg, but this restriction utterly missed the point. I knew that I had to stay away from Diana and her friends. There was still a volcano; I was not finished.

The rest of the spring was unendurable. Whenever I would recall my Diana-related conduct—all my conduct— from the hayride onward, I became wincingly ashamed. I wanted to kill or to banish everybody and everything that reminded me of my shame, but it was impossible. My shame permeated everything, because Diana permeated everything. If she moved away, if I moved away, if she died, if I died, it would make no difference. She had already occurred. She could grow, but she could not be diminished. She would be equally alive in me (she is) whether physically absent or physically present. The only survivable course was to heal over outwardly, to moderate my behavior by the will, to learn to deny. But the only motivation for doing that, I knew, was to build a more substantial base from which to renew my quest for Diana. And that quest was already hopeless. I had spoiled it myself. I fell and fell. Several years later in high school when I read—not in its own text but in a short story by J. D. Salinger—the opening lines of Eliot's "Waste Land,"

> April is the cruelest month,
> Breeding lilacs out of the dead land,
> Mixing memory with desire

I had the first of a continuing series of realizations that the right words for one's own experience have invariably been written already, perfectly.

Sometimes exhausted with the monotony of longing, with not having, I would practice giving up. I would tell myself: *It is over. It is not coming back. This absence is the truth.* Then I would wait. Without fail Diana images would come crowding into consciousness: her temple against my cheek, Diana nestled close to me in the cold of the hay wagon, her voice, her script, her smile on the brink, her fingers closing over mine. I remember no days from this time, only nights. It was a windy, noisy, spring. External noises—crickets, the wind in the trees, traffic—produced a faintly familiar effect on me: the sounds seemed to playing *through* me, as though I were some kind of musical instrument. I cannot have slept much. Over and over, in the maddening repetitions of half sleep, I pictured the swirling branches outside my bedroom window touching the tips of adjacent branches, these brushing against other branches in an unbroken pathway of hisses and rushes between my window and Diana's.

There were occasional, brief moments when I had Diana again, when memory superseded present reality. At such moments she was nearby writing my name, and I, the funniest, trickiest boy in the school, could do anything I pleased. Then with a start I would be restored fully to my loss.

By school's end and the onset of summer, it was clear that I must somehow harden against my hurt or cease to matter at all. One clear breezy day as I lay resting on the concrete border of the town swimming pool, I heard somebody a towel or two away say something in praise of Diana. Without thinking I spoke up: "Who cares?" I listened to my own words hanging in the air. I would be able to manage more of this, it occurred to me. I could manage it if I could

145

somehow dislodge her from the center of my consciousness. I needed to hurt her a little, not in the deeper, hopeless sense of showing her my love, but in the practical sense of demoting myself from "special friend" to "enemy." The distinction was meaningless to me—no, I preferred enemy—and if it meant anything to Diana (as if she were capable of enmity), tough. I was tough that summer. I became deftly sarcastic. I learned the outrageous effrontery of words detached from sentiment: how to say "oh" and "good" and "that's nice" and "I like it" and mean "I don't care." Not caring was beckoningly appealing. I took it up with little resistance and, not for the last time, stepped down voluntarily into a stratum of diminished perception. I became ordinary.

Then one leaden gray afternoon along the Lake Michigan dunes, having strayed off from a swimming party to skip stones over the waves, I became aware of a cluster of girl swimmers being pulled gradually in my direction by the current. When they reached a point where I was either going to have to move farther down the beach or stop throwing stones, I realized that one of them was Diana. I had not recognized her earlier in her bathing cap. I was certain she was aware of me. I skipped a stone practically in their midst. There were squeals of protest. I skipped another. They turned and began treading back toward the rest of the party. Bobbing indignantly away from me in their bathing caps, they looked a little like ducks. I skipped another stone. It slapped the skin of the water and glided up again in a low arc that passed within an inch or two of Diana's mouth; I was sure that it was going to hit her. She stopped, took a few steps toward shore. I knew this would be hard for her.

"Ricky," she asked me, full of concern, "What are you trying to do?"

"Maybe you could just get out of my way," I said and threw a stone as far as I could into the lake.

146

That closed the door for a time. And for a few years I experienced myself passively becoming a good citizen, first of the junior high school, then the high school. Sometimes, for weeks, I experienced myself as a fragment, sometimes as a man of great age installed cruelly amid the meaningless chattering of children. But all the while there remained the sacred door.

Half-awake, I asked girls to dances, bought them corsages, dined in restaurants, thanked them for their time. The characteristic awkwardness and reticence I presented to the girls I called on and to their parents was actually the public face of deep grief. I kissed some of the girls, held them close to me, examined and compared their bodies. I became objective about each new sensation; though often enough aroused, I refused to be worshipful. With the same objectivity I let myself enter into, then fall out of, privileged arrangements with various girls. Sometimes there was a stirring intimation of a new *otherness* in a girl I was "going with," but I closed myself off reflexively to any such risk or effort. Instead I directed my romantic relationships, as if from a deep interior headquarters, on the principle of creating partial, manageable Dianas. I liked some of the girls for the familiar angularity of their faces. I liked others for the Diana-like timbre of their voices. I pursued one girl for a while because her name was Diana. I was inclined favorably to girls—and to anybody else—who lived on the north side of town. After many brief arrangements and rearrangements (do parents know there are dozens of these?), I became paired with a "steady" girl for nearly all of the high school years. Blond, soft featured, with an understated intellect hard as a diamond, she was not at all a Diana look-alike, but like Diana she seemed naturally aligned, in a way I could only partially grasp, with Goodness itself. This was a little unsettling for me, and for reasons I did not understand

147

myself, I would periodically provoke this lovely girl: embarrass her, mock her, fail to arrive. She was astonished.

Of course Diana continued to move—to move prominently—through the physical world we shared. She was very popular and through the transforming power of her self-effacement was regularly elected to lead the school. Everything I had created—my new citizenship, my attainments, my dangerous "wit"—was a lead shield against the radiation of her beauty. For in fact I still felt the glow of her all over school, all over town. I did not take her classes, did not serve in her organizations. I clammed up, avoided contact with even the forbidding angels who were her friends—I was inordinately aware of *their* movements also. Unavoidably, I would encounter her in a corridor or, after a party, would find that we were to be driven home in the same car. Down dropped the lead casings. She spoke to me always with great care and kindness. I answered her as an absence: "Oh," "good," "that's nice."

By the time I had become a practiced teenager, now finishing high school, I began to relax my precautions against experiencing Diana too intensely. I let myself think about her. I allowed myself, selectively, to remember. I can see now that this was a necessary part of my preparation to leave school and to leave town. Rather more potently, I came to dwell increasingly in two highly specific fantasies in which Diana and I were reunited in a remote future. In the first, *I am walking to her house in the rain. It is night, and I am just turning away from the traffic lights of the highway onto her street. The collar of my trench coat is pulled up against the rain. I am twenty-nine years old and have been through something or achieved something that has left me unalterably determined. I look up to see lights in the windows of her house. I am expected.* There is a disjunction, then: *We are sitting in the front seat of a black Renault. It is night and snowing thickly. We both peer ahead intently as the wipers clear snow away from clouded V's of the windshield. We are stopped in traffic, about to enter Montreal. Our suitcases are in the back seat. Something upsetting has happened. We have no clear plans. Diana takes my hand.* The other fantasy is more compact, more a single image. *It is a bright noon in a seaside village, although the sea cannot be seen. I am standing, bearded, perhaps forty, painting at an easel set up in the tiny front lawn of a cottage. I have rented the cottage, and the door is open. Inside all is dark and disorder: there is a rumpled bed, tubes of paint, and many canvases. There are dark bottles of liquor everywhere. Diana approaches the cottage. She has found me after a long search. She is very tired. I recognize her and turn to greet her. I am holding a drink in my hand.* I found both of these *tableaux* inexpressibly alluring. Twenty-nine, forty—the idea of changing, of time actually passing, began to come alive with promise. Something within me that had been deadened began to unfurl. Then, before I could stop it, it was out: Diana. It was the original desire, the same desire, rampant.

I went straight to Diana. (I alone in the school understood the sudden break with my long-standing "steady.") I could not have Diana, but I could fall in love with the quest for her. I would be resilient. I felt radically reoriented to her in love. I wondered what had so terrified me about rejection. Rejected already, I was willing to be rejected every waking minute. I asked Diana to the prom, and she accepted.

My personal aspirations for this (final) Dance were for once appropriate: I wanted to avoid being a spectacular fool. Censor and editor were in place. (What was actually in place was something hard won: a responsible regard for the quality of Diana's evening.) It was tacitly acknowledged that Diana and I had reached a special "understanding"—but I did not know what it was. What I did understand was that I was under solemn obligation to behave like a Boy at a Dance, which involved nothing more onerous than feeling that a foot or two of cotton insulated me from the world moving about me.

My preparations had assumed the Diana of memory, not the Diana of the Prom Dress. She appeared in her living room in a dress of such simplicity, of a cloth so cleanly and astringently white, it glowed. And of course Diana glowed. Already on arrival I had failed. I became at once a spectacular fool (and only my giddy awareness that I was saved me).

"You're not a girl!" I told her excitedly as soon as we left her house, then quickly explained that I meant she was now a woman.

Diana West was so beautiful, standing close to me in the required attitudes of dance, or standing apart, her profile at my side, that she passed in and out of pure objectivity. Only when she was a portrait (a Sargent) of a beautiful young woman in white could I really see her. "Ricky," she said to me in a laugh. "You are looking at me very hard." For a joke I assumed the spastic stance of a gaping lunatic (but I continued to look).

It was working. Even through the cotton, happily, it was working. It was not romance, but it was gently pleasant. It was acting the part of one of those benign ghosts of stage comedies who bears only amusingly on the principals. It was the laughing prom; conversations were carried out in the uncountable modalities of laughter. It was weirdly instructive playing this ghost-jester. Whereas when I had intentionally diminished myself in a direction *away* from Diana, I felt oppressively of this world, heavy with the here and now. But by contrast, when I diminished myself *in* Diana's direction, I felt light, pleasingly insubstantial, and—this was new—*full of goodwill.*

After the dance we changed clothes for the next rounds

of amusements: a slow train, pulsing with music and games, had been hired for those of us who paid for it, up to a resort in southern Wisconsin, where we could have breakfast, stroll over the greensward, paddle over its water courses, entrain for home, and collapse. All of this was less good, a darker, heavier dream. Diana and I found the only profoundly quiet compartment on the train. Could it have been as dark and quiet as I remember? If only we hadn't become detached from the revelers. I felt my insulation begin to dissolve away. Knowing it was hopeless, recalling all the long, dark falling that would follow the attempt, I wanted to hold her. Diana knew that I wanted to and ached sympathetically. I willed myself from her side and moved to the seat facing her. The train rocked and swayed, emphasizing the quiet. Neither of us slept. We might have said more than this, but whatever it was, it was expressed in the only exchange I can remember:

I said, "I haven't known you for a long time."

"I know," she said, "but we know each other pretty well."

"I would like to know you much better," I said, trespassing, losing control.

"Oh, I know you do," she said with deep sympathy. "But would you please understand?"

I thought I understood already (but I did not). There was Diana, and she was love. You open up to love like a wound, and you spilled ecstatically out of yourself. Free-floating after love, you realized you were not really good enough for it. You were tiny, mean-spirited, too personal. Then you began to fall away. I remember looking across the silence at Diana and trying to reduce her to her material elements: her tennis shoes, her wool trousers, her sweater, the set of her lips, the bones of her face, the crush of her dark hair against the seat cushion. It did not work. She was greater than the sum of her parts. Love worked through her,

151

not in her. If she fell asleep (she didn't) and wheezed (she didn't), and awoke with a blemish erupted on her cheek (it didn't), she would have grown in love and beauty. At sunrise, bone-weary as soldiers returning from combat, we left the train and walked over dewy, misty lawns, down forest paths over which mist hung in clouds over all but the bottom branches. Dimly aware of the shapes of others, we walked and walked through this land of the dead. When the first bird sang, the prom was over.

I did not "understand" that night on the train, but in hearing Diana's appeal I did, I think, turn one notch of the celestial wheel toward understanding. Until the prom I was driven entirely, and in perfect failure, by the desire to possess, not to understand. Even my flawed attempt to limit this urge helped me to see that, however consuming and powerful, Possession was an urge among many urges; it was not the only orientation to love.

That summer I was an alien wherever I went. Having grown gigantically out of its rows of desks, I was finished with school. In the fall I would enter college in New England. (New England was in the family of beloved place-dreams that included Denver and Montreal.) I was also about to be finished with the town, so by day I worked, shirtless, tending the shrubs and facilities of its parks. By night, often all night, I walked its settled streets, mapping them securely into the grooves of memory. Working in solitude in the windy parks, I considered the merits of my life in this town as a story. Something had happened to me: love. There had been Diana. There had been loss and fury and a million wrong answers. What was the meaning of the one right answer? Could it *be* the right answer, devoid of love's feeling? What had Diana wanted when she had urged me to "understand?" It became the only question left in town.

That summer when the rest of my family switched off

152

their lamps for the night, I would arise quietly, let myself out the cellar door and walk the deserted streets. In the combined streetlight and moonlight, the lawns were silver-blue. The walkways were heavily fragrant with swollen shrubs. Late at night the earth, even pavement, softens beneath one's feet. It is possible to walk for hours, for miles without tiring.

Inevitably one night I let myself be pulled northward up into the network of streets charged with Diana. Just as inevitably I awoke to find myself stopped on the walk in front of her house, looking up into the darkened windows of her room. I looked down the walk to my right, in the direction in which, eleven years hence, in my fantasy, I would be approaching in the rain. It was perfectly imaginable: there *could* be access to the waking world from the dreaming world. *I look up and see light in the windows of Diana's house. I am expected.*

I walked around to the back of the house and reclined on the backyard grass to consider all of this. There was nothing to consider. Diana was sleeping in one bricked-in cell of this house, and I loved her. I could see no point in feeling this and not saying it. It was possible, by hoisting my hip up onto the brick window ledge of the garage, to get a foothold. Then by rising very carefully, I could extend a hand up over the gutter and pull myself up to a standing position. From this height I could reach the base of a wooden railing, which enclosed (what was until then) a decorative balcony. With a wild upward swing of the leg, I scrambled and slithered over the edge of the roof, then over the railing.

I moved to Diana's window and drew a fingernail over the screen. While the lights from the street illuminated the garage roof to the extent that my movements cast dark shadows over the brickwork, it was impossible to see anything through Diana's screen. I scratched for a while longer, then whistled in imitation of what I thought might be a night bird. Then I made a few deep-throated whines in the manner of a cat.

Diana's face appeared suddenly at the screen.

"Ricky," she whispered, "what are you doing up here?"

I told her I had just been passing by and decided to stop. She laughed. She was in no hurry. I could stay. I wanted to stay until it got light.

"Ricky," she said, "it's three o'clock. Did you want something?"

It was time to unburden myself. I could see that this encounter was what had drawn me outdoors each night for hours cross-hatching the town. I told her I had a message for her.

She waited. But I could not speak. I could feel myself falling away in the old hopelessness, only this hopelessness would be final. If only one of the great exhalations of my love could just attach itself to her, would stick, there would be no need to say anything. She was only a few inches away through the screen.

"What is the message?" she asked, already melancholy in anticipation.

I began rummaging through my pockets. There was no message in my pockets. But I found a scrap of something, a matchbook or a golf card.

"It's right here," I said, holding the scrap some distance from the screen. "Can you read it?"

"No, I can't," whispered Diana. "Why don't you read it to me?"

Why was I up on this roof in the middle of the night? With light-of-day clarity, I loathed myself. I willed myself vanished, far across town. *Say something,* I told myself, *just say it again and vanish.*

"It says," I spoke in a wavering boy's voice, "I—love—you."

A long pause, however thoughtful on Diana's part, would have been the most complete derision possible, would have opened the way to my own self-derision. But Diana spoke at once.

"Bless you. I know you do. Your love is *wonderful*. And I know someday you are going to find out what it is for."

"I know what it's for," I said, but I was filling time. My thoughts were swirling. I did not know anything.

"No, you just think you do," said Diana. Then, "It is very late. My father gets up pretty soon. You go home and go to sleep."

"When can I see you again?"

"Go to sleep, Ricky."

"When can—" Her screen was dark. I dropped down from the garage roof, awkwardly, a jackknifed length of gutter in my wake.

Your love is wonderful . . . someday you are going to find out what it is for. Love for something? Love for "something" other than Diana? It was too hard to understand. And with that admission I began to understand.

To Diana West (the girl in the bed in the house) I owe the only liberty worth having: the liberty of seeing that beloved persons are those who by grace have been aligned with Goodness itself. Goodness in persons is love. The world is teeming with Dianas, once we have been hurt sufficiently free of our own selfishness to see them. If Diana West had not helped me, had she, due to some perfectly allowable personal need, loved me back physically and conventionally, Love could not have been so fully (and so painfully) disclosed to me. I would have been stuck on the equation, Love = ♥ Diana. I would not have had the joy of recognizing so much

155

of love's variety in the world beyond the north side. Nor is it imaginable that I would have found my wife, a woman of miraculously true alignment, a woman inexpressibly soft of skin and pure of scent, if I had been damned to be forever peering through the cloudy windshield at a dreamscape of Montreal, or at any other celestial no place in the failed pursuit of Diana West.

A woman friend of mine who corresponds from Chicago has seen Diana West recently. She mentioned it briefly to me in a letter: . . . "Diana was there, luminous as always."

A Story
Comes True

Childhood is alive with vivid promises. There is no adult counterpart to the condition. Adulthood is actual, and it is essential, but it is never, from the standpoint of the emerging adult, desirable. Beware of all children, adolescents, and even young men and women who are on all occasions suitably dressed and well behaved. They are desperate. And if ever a teenager begins talking about the advantages of this or that college in terms of the edge it will confer later in accounting or medicine, step into his path. Seize him and shake him until he is senseless. This is a spiritual suicide, well advanced.

I did not wish to become an adult. Adulthood was for me a "finished" condition, and I could not imagine being finished. I felt, rather, like a character in a story. It was a good story—full of dark portents and flashes of promise—but a story still in progress. For some reason, the narrative was irritatingly stalled. Up to this point, my personal story had been sympathetically connected to the sustaining stories of my boyhood reading. These stories had told me, literally, who I was. Now it was hard to tell. I needed a new story badly.

The first story, as I have said, was Christmas. The next was the tale of the tailor who killed seven with one blow. I was three or four when my mother read it to me from an oversize fairy-tale "treasury" that may have come from her own childhood library. There was one glossily colored illustration, printed on a separate creamy page, for each tale, and it seemed to me that once I knew the story, all of its elements could be evoked through deep immersion in the picture. I loved the tailor because he used his wits and bits of cheese to get so much more than he deserved. That was me—and perhaps every other soul on earth: poised on edge, expecting, often against an avalance of likelihood, to get more than he or she deserves.

As soon as I could read stories for myself, I began reading in the direction of Jack London. I read volumes of his adventure stories and his animal books, but they all came down to one story, *The Call of the Wild*, and *Call of the Wild* came down to one moment: when, after he avenges the death of his murdered master, the dog-hero Buck is free to rejoin the inexhaustible North out of which he evolved. Only an animal, I realized, could be granted such a privilege: to return to the love-sense prior to consciousness.

For me, these vaulting spiritual reminders in print were almost uncomfortably stirring, but they were also very private. Increasingly, as I forayed tentatively into school and community, they did not bear on daily waking life. But when I fell under the sway of Claire Bee's Chip Hilton sports series, the myth-feeling at last merged with a complete, believable social order, including a region, a town, a school, an agreeable network of friends, and a household. Valley Falls, Indiana, the setting of these wonderfully paced football, basketball, and baseball stories, could be plotted on a real map. Chip Hilton's stamina, resourcefulness, and adherence to fair play—lessons abundantly available in the *Odyssey* and Arthurian stories—played themselves out in a credible contemporary setting, in *history*. Far from bringing daily business "down to earth," the Chip Hilton series elevated ordinary experience up into the vibrant realm of story. The drama of sport and of sportsmen like Chip Hilton could transform, I believed, every particular thing it touched. This realization cast my waking experience in fresh light. I became observant. I became curious. There were stories everywhere.

But this imaginative passage into "real life" events and settings became eventually a kind of descent. The mythic realm is spare and bright; the naturalistic world is crowded and dark. Like millions of other emerging adolescents, I was at first surprised and then gladly carried away by a doomed angel of the dark and crowded world. He was Holden Caulfield of *Catcher in the Rye*. His New York City was a vividly particular as Chip Hilton's Valley Falls, but, although there are flashes of beauty (mostly remembered) in Holden's world, there is everywhere the suggestion that the world is spoiled. A *spoiled* world, a spoiled life—this was news to me. Poor Holden, too: a terrible student, dumped into and out of schools, on the verge of trouble at home, and no imaginable future.

Holden's appealing, almost paranormal sensitivity to other souls is not quite enough to sustain him in the waking world, yet one cannot help cheering him on in his erratic quest for essentials. At first I found myself admiring

Holden's ineffectuality and weakness as much as I did Chip's strength. Only later would I realize that it wasn't weakness at all.

After I read *Catcher in the Rye,* Holden's story seemed to be the only story there was. I could not forget it, and its main effect on me was to raise doubts about my personal future. I began to go about seeking wounds, and I found plenty. I continued to read, desperate for a new, healing story, but I did not find one. In Dickens's coming-of-age stories, especially *Great Expectations,* I sometimes thought I detected Holden's angel making his way and even thriving in a world teeming with pompous minor officials, hapless thespians, and oafs. But there was something too bemused, too artful, and too safe about Dickens to help me. I was lost.

For a time I think I stopped believing that a story, any story, could be really true. I could not locate either the God-sense or the love-sense and was growing increasingly numb to anything of the kind. It took an accident to reconnect me. A teacher assigned John Keats's "The Eve of St. Agnes," and I was vaulted longingly back to where I belonged. There is a moment early in the poem when the virgin Madeline, impatient to leave a household celebration, stands in the festive midst of "music yearning like a God in pain." That is exactly what it took to catch my attention: "music yearning like a God in pain." But at last, I realized, here was a *story.*

Keats's poem is a sure, single flash of love: language aligned with the beauty it celebrates. Madeline and her lover Porphyro are Romeo and Juliet, compact as a gem. "The Eve of St. Agnes" drugged me, made a fool out of me. Love itself seemed to shimmer within its imagery. Why, I wondered, had I forsaken this? And for what?

But there was still a problem. For although Keats, mythology, and certain classical paintings could arouse the old feeling of connectedness my first stories had produced, the experience was a kind of emotional retreat, a surprising memory. What was there to connect me to present reality? To a suburban neighborhood, to a school? What was the point of these disturbing glimpses into an overwhelmingly rich and bright world if we have to spend practically all of our time in another one which, by contrast, is so monotonous and dim? Was there a *story* about this? Perhaps the answer did not take story form; perhaps it required disciplined learning: scholarship.

But as I have said already, I was in no condition to undertake a disciplined study of anything. I think I was afraid of what I would find if I finished. I could not bear to be "finished," in life or death. So I began to make a point of not finishing anything. I declined to start anything that ended, and I declined to finish anything I started. This is one way of saying no to the waking world, but it does not buy time.

By the time I was an undergraduate, I was sick and sinking fast. Free now of even the token restraints of household membership, I found any restraint intolerable, even the most uncontestedly justifiable responsibilities. When my clothes and bedding needed laundering, I bought new things. When I ran out of money to buy them, I used my roommates'. When they complained, I stayed in bed.

But deep inside my whale's torpor pulsed the metabolism of a shrew.

If you stay in bed long enough, you go into a cocoon. You begin observing others as characters in a film without sound. You hear voices as if from under water. The will is drawn back into its source, and then you have no will. I became so sleepy that my blood, urine, heart, and lungs had to be checked repeatedly. Only one thing seemed to sustain me, to jackknife me out of the supine: intimacy.

Colleges are organized residentially to be like honeycombs. In every cell there are one, two, three or more souls,

161

many of them shrews like me, moving about, chattering, rustling papers, bunching cloth. There are hundreds of cells in every building, and there are dozens of buildings. It became essential for me to catalog every shrew and all the other animals. Beginning at nightfall, and sometimes continuing long into bright day. I began my cycles of burrowing about the cells. I may not have been a self for a time. I may have had a collective existence of a very low order: termite or mole-rat.

But there was nothing there. Collectivity beckons, but it cannot quite be realized. We are selves, even in flight. The intimacy of fellow shrews always peters out just when one is most desperate for it. Somebody's conversation flags in the dawn light. Somebody has a practical obligation—to visit a dying relative, to take an exam. People turn out to be irrevocably tied to the waking world, turn out not to have been shrews in the first place. Some nights I would vacate cell after cell, leaving only sleepers in my wake. All I did was talk—jab, tease, set up nonsense systems for the pleasure of subjecting them to close analysis—but there was never enough of it. Even at three A.M., seated in the midst of a yattering, babbling cellful of shrews, there was not enough of it. I knew in advance that somebody would tire of laughing and would fall asleep. The sun would come up. Future district managers and engineers would begin filling the shower stalls. They would engage in the inconceivable mystery of breakfast, then stream across the campus walks to classes.

I watched a hundred sunrises by myself. Then I would sink into the heaviness of my cocoon, sleeping through a balanced program of arts and sciences.

Where was I? Where did I go? Wherever it was, the God-sense, the love-sense, and all the old stories were, I knew, still true. But they somehow did not reach, did not

162

penetrate into the cocoon. It was easy to be sick. I was practically always sick. To have died then would have barely mattered. It would have mattered as much as the passing of a shrew.

It never occurred to me to master one of the organized bodies of knowledge the college preserved and perpetuated. Even before college I knew these were not for me. The earliest realization of my unsuitability for the standard disciplines occurred in the course of my high school chemistry class. It was clear that school chemistry was not going to be the bewitching transformation of matter that had thrilled me as a younger boy. It was a course about language and about making models. Sticks like Tinkertoys were joined together with colored wooden bulbs (to suggest organic bonding) to form "molecules." For me these embarrassing Tinkertoy contraptions representing chemical essences were emblematic of chemistry itself. The labs were no better. In pretended fussiness we were to measure, mix, count, and weigh bits of solution to demonstrate an abstract relationship among the chemicals. The relationship was expressed in a number carried out to many decimal places. Children learn more thinning paint and stirring soup. One series of "experiments" involved the formation of butyric acid, the rancid smell of which sent me racing from the lab. A block away, sitting on somebody's front stoop, I considered the hard-edge facade of the high school rising over the tree line. *Why had I been born into such an age?*

Chemistry also posed the first intellectual exercises I could not master immediately. My prior classroom experiences had taught me that teachers and the materials they distributed were pitched to wide-eyed primitives, to a race capable of repeating very basic lineal sequences, but who, unfortunately, arose each day with all previous knowledge erased. The units of the chemistry text were also pitched to

163

this race, but pitched in such a way as to confound them. A week of class was devoted to each chapter of the text. On Fridays an examination was given on the material covered in the chapter. The tests were standardized (produced by the company that published the text), and questions were answered by darkening in one of four or five circles adjacent to rival answers on the prepared answer sheet. I was startled, after three or four introductory weeks of chemistry, that I could not, with confidence, answer *any* of the questions on the weekly exams. I began to read the text and experienced the novel disorientation of being unable to make sense of a single word. The sound of the words—even familiar words—and their images would be taken up into the antechamber of consciousness, would flicker about for a few seconds, then fly off. Words combined in certain ways, I realized, failed to cohere into statements. Perhaps this was true only of chemistry.

I was too competitive, too prideful at that time, not to master chemistry, at least not to master it outwardly. Repetition, I determined, was the key. Lying in bed, I would read the chapter, blink absently at the ceiling for a time (for a minute or two, for an entire Sunday afternoon?), then read it again, and so on. This was a deadening, grueling process, like carrying a heavy object in one's arms for far too long. But the result was fascinating. Out of the blur of the chapter's prose and formulas and tables would emerge the outline of something not quite distinct. The impression was like what emerges on a photographic plate halfway between blankness and a fully realized image, like a shoreline approached through fog. These shadowy contours would appear after my third consecutive reading and could not be clarified by further readings. But the shadows were enough for the standardized exams. On Friday mornings I recognized each blurry contour and darkened in the adjacent circle. I felt not

164

fully sighted and a bit dishonest doing this ghost work. Did the other good chemistry students "understand" chemistry this way? Then, in a chill, I began to wonder if perhaps they might understand all of their subjects in this manner. I began to be suspicious of "performance" as a measure of anything substantial. I did not care to perform in the land of the dead.

But by the time I was insulated deep inside my undergraduate cocoon, every subject—the classroom itself—had become the land of the dead. I remember with real sadness losing control of biology, which had begun so brightly for me. Classification of plants and animals satisfied a deep need for hierarchy. I accepted gladly the order in so much complexity. I had nothing but reverence for the courage and gritty ingenuity of biological selection. Biology itself seemed at first reverent: attempting no more than to keep track of processes so particular no one could have guessed them. The human systems were most magnificent. The subtle checks and balances of the endocrine system, the infinite complexities and adaptabilities of nervous system transactions seemed worthy of a lifetime's study on the part of a good man or woman. Respiration, circulation, reproduction—these were the wheels of bodily life. Every organ was as distinctive as the nations of Europe, even such expendable balkans as the gallbladder and appendix. I had half a mind to tend these organs myself, to be a physician.

But then the thrust of biology shifted decisively to molecules. The subordinate, and to my mind monotonous, economies of cells and parts of cells became the sole focus of study. In just a few weeks the sense of connectedness in life was gone. The professors were after something exclusive, something very small that was important because it was not easily accessible. The human spirit, including its intelligence, is not naturally aroused by a structural concept like "molecule"; I began to wonder whether molecular biology is

165

not carried on by people who want the power to change matter at an elemental level, perhaps even to hurt it. There is no wonder in molecules to compare with the wonder of what they compose. Who can honestly be distracted from an orchid or a python or an owl to ask after its molecules? Perhaps ghost people can, savants who respond to patterns of life as I responded to ghost patterns in my chemistry book.

I lost the will for biology, and before long I had lost the will for everything. I remember that in the period of my deepest malaise, I was enrolled in a course in economics. (I must have been enrolled in three or four other courses as well, but emotionally they all came down to economics.) I was too passive and sick to care much about it, but even in my objectivity, I found economics something of a marvel. Whereas I believe chemistry is a real body of knowledge (knowledge about real things) and only a ghost science when viewed through personal mists, economics seems to be *inherently* a ghost science, no matter how it is viewed. In philosophy and theology, many things are reduced to a few things, then these to the one thing that is true. In economics everything is reduced to a few things, but they can be anything: supply, demand, scarcity, labor, an invisible hand.

My study of economics was not helped much by my brain's being organized in an unusual pattern of so-called mixed-dominance. I am left-eyed, right-footed, and ambidextrous in many things, although I eat and play golf only right-handed, throw a ball and swing a bat only left-handed. When I play the piano, right and left hands sometimes become wily contestants, each set on out-embellishing the other. If I am given right-left directions too suddenly while driving in traffic, my mind is purged violently of all thought, and I proceed ahead without turning either way, my jaws locked tightly. Similarly, in tennis any ball approaching me at an angle corresponding to the right-left axis of my cerebral

166

hemispheres causes me to extend my racket straight out in front of me while I undergo a passing, but unpleasant, seizure. I also frequently say and think the precise opposite of what I mean, and I am irritated when I am not immediately understood.

These right-left confusions are more frequent when I am tired, which was my chronic condition as an undergraduate, never more so than when I was enrolled in economics. The ghost science of economics is organized around a number of paired concepts—supply and demand, cost and benefit, fixed and variable costs, etc. Sometimes the pairs behave like opposites, sometimes like dependent and independent variables, sometime like cause and effect. The pairs can behave in these ways interchangeably and simultaneously. It is possible to graph one element of the pair in terms of the other—or in terms of any and all other elements one chooses. But sufferers of mixed dominance are apt to reverse the axes of their graphs. (The truth of the matter is that for mixed-dominant people, graphs of any kind are neither conceptual nor visual aids; they are invitations to epilepsy.) I was in addition prone to say "supply" when I meant "demand," and so on with the other linked pairs. Even when carefully coached about how to calculate what would happen to specific variables in the national economy when a related variable was altered, my response in examinations was either too many directions in traffic or tennis ball right at me.

Economics is probably the only science that would accommodate my particular liabilities. "What would be the foreseeable effect on the industrial Northeast if there were a sustained embargo on oil produced outside the United States?" Of course the correct answer is that any number of things could happen. They could happen exclusively, serially, or all at once. In fact there is *nothing that might not happen* if oil were no longer being imported. Price of existing stores could skyrocket, due to scarcity and necessity. People with elastic incomes would get it all, unless those with inelastic incomes got there first. Price of existing stores could also drop to nothing, as motorists (like me) would grow discouraged at so much uncertainty and stop driving altogether. Victory gardens would proliferate wildly—or disappear from the landscape almost overnight. Radio listening and record-playing would rise sharply among the newly unemployed, then, sympathetically, among the employed. *An economy without oil?* Without automotive fuel? Without fuel to heat and to cool? Without internal combustion of any kind? Without mowed grass? Without paint? Without plastics? The answer is easy: the economy would slow to an agonizing halt. Or, just as easily, it would be wonderfully invigorated, turning away from oil altogether, capturing sunlight itself in panels of glass, in heaps of granite, in cork, in upholstery, on the upturned faces of bathers.

Sick as I was and mixed-dominant, I did well in economics. I would go on to teach it for three years, winning praise for conceptual clarity and quantitative precision.

Silliness is not harmless; it can be one of the faces of sickness. Silliness was doing its part, I believe, to kill me. I grew weaker by the day, by the semester. I stopped running, stopped skiing. Then I stopped being able to imagine running or skiing. I remember feeling inexplicably proud of myself one day because I had arisen from bed, showered, and dressed myself.

I slept through classes, through deadlines, through the meals my parents had paid for. Occasionally I would arise in a panic of guilt, make my way to a class where the parliamentary system of Canada or Yeats's love for Maude Gonne was being discussed. Frantic at my alienation from the discussion, I would raise my hand and unleash a stream of gibberish that brought the classroom to an embarrassed

168

hush. The anxiety dream—so widely shared—of searching for an elusive class or examination for which none of one's obligations have been met was my reality, both waking and sleeping.

Required for some reason to address the college newspaper staff and its guests in the dining room of the local inn, I inadvertently got drunk over cocktails and could barely make my way into the dining room. Seated at the head of the table, I lapsed in and out of coherence, perhaps slept. At one point during the meal there was some excitement about a bat that had been disturbed and that was fluttering about the far corner of the dining room. This seemed important. I arose awkwardly from my chair, upsetting a tureen of gravy onto the tablecloth and onto the lap of the wife of the dean of students. I said I would find some more gravy and left the table, intending to locate the bat, determined to kill it. I slept on the village green. I stopped brushing my teeth. I wanted only to sleep. For more than two years my chest cavity felt as though it were unwilling to expand for air. Some days I would awake gasping for life's breath.

I refused to die. Deep within, the shrew was performing the frenzied acrobatics of a lunatic. I began to ache in my torpor. I began to look for a way out of bed. There can be nothing more arduous than reversing the course of withdrawal from waking life. Indolence, denial, and flight convey one into the cocoon faster than one can fall. But the laws of character development are strict and invariable. Whereas extensive periods of discipline, obedience, and goodwill create no special resistance to sliding immediately backward into sloth and selfishness, every increment of the latter diminishes by an exponential factor the likelihood of achieving any of the former. The prospect of self-improvement is more than difficult; it is impossible. (I slept on this conclusion.) I have always understood the recovering alcoholic's

169

credo: "one day at a time." A day is a long time to live by the will. Alcoholics do not claim to be able to do it without help. In their own way alcoholics have been to the bed.

I had to get out. Indicative of my character at the time, I looked for a shortcut. Indicative of my intelligence at the time was the shortcut I took. Because I was technically and geographically a college student, and because I had learned nothing there, I resolved to become encyclopedic. This had the right feeling of penance about it, also the reassuring futility necessary to sustain the hope of a young man in bed. I would introject the world, element by element, into my head and it would be mine.

From the very start, my impulse to encyclopedic knowledge led me on a course of unrelieved doubt and anguish, but it did wake me up. Not knowing where to start, I started grandiosely at the beginning of human history—at the "dawn of civilization," as the textbooks say. But I could not find it for all the texts and "earliest" documents in the world. (The problem was that I wanted newspaper accounts, not the Genesis story or the theogeny of Hesiod or Ovid, the inviting simplicity of which kept floating overhead in great diaphanous bubbles.) I read the transcriptions of the earliest writings from the Fertile Crescent. The very oldest were partial lists of goods: gums, cloth, crockery. There were fragments of tribute to the everlasting divinity of pharaohs and other god-kings long gone. There were more lists: comparative harvest yields, livestock counts, balances of payments. Later, in earliest Egypt, there were some complaints, preserved in hieroglyph, about the young and about the degeneracy of the times: drinking, thievery, the shoddiness of workmanship. In Thebes, in Babylon, in Troy, in Knossos— it was the same everywhere. I could not pick up the thread of a story.

I deserted chronology and went after great lives. But like so many others who have sought history this way, I was overcome with anxiety at so much choice. I would no sooner pick up a life of Alexander and read the account of his father then begin to unravel with doubt: what do I know about *Philip of Macedon?* What do I know about *Macedon?* About *Hellas* for that matter? About any of its founders and shapers? Don't Herodotus and Thucydides tell about that? What do I know about *Herodotus* and *Thucydides?* Before (I am now thankful) I would reach the references to Alexander's tutor, *Aristotle,* I would be clawing ancient history volumes down from the library shelf with the desperation of a burglar. The first chapter of every book pointed to my obvious need of more background. *Where does one get background?* This is the most profound question in scholarship.

I abandoned my researches into the early chapters of the accounts of great lives. For a time I looked for security in the work of great synthesizers, of historians whose interpretation of the past might provide an intelligible context for everything particular I would need to know. I plowed into Gibbon, Hegel, Toynbee, even into Will and Ariel Durant. I tried, like a bettor with a hot tip, the *psycho*histories of Erik Erikson and lesser lights. But these meat grinders only led me back to the meat. For some reason I was disinclined to believe a word of their vaulting generalities until I knew what happened in the first place. *I* needed to know what Caesar did, and *I* needed to know how one found out what Caesar had done. Back I went to the great lives, back to the partial lists of ancient inventories, all the while my lack of background opening up like the busy panorama of history itself.

My labors were never the slightest bit satisfying. After a day or two lost in accounts of early monasticism (eremitic and cenobitic), someone at dinner would mention Rasputin, and I would twirl off into a frenzy. What did I know about Rasputin? About the *Romanovs?* There was, I realized sickeningly, *all of Russia* to do. The pursuit of Russia would send me off crazily into the eleventh-century conversion of the Russians to Byzantine Orthodoxy. With my finger I followed Vikings up mapped rivers to the Slavic settlements they raided. I traced Turks and Greeks up into Russia's soft underbelly. But what did I know about *Vikings?* About *Turks?* There was all of *Islam* to do. The next day I would turn a familiar corner in the college library and there would be a seemingly newly erected stand of metal shelving holding more than a lifetime's reading in *art history.* I had forgotten about all the monuments and pictures.

Walking to a meal or climbing the dormitory stairs, it would occur to me that I did not know the capitals of every state. The geography of sub-Saharan Africa was a blur. I did not know even the rudiments of Buddhism or Taoism. How had I ignored so many central languages? I needed to know French, Italian, Spanish, and German, but first I had to learn Greek, Hebrew, Arabic, and Sanskrit. I also needed to know Russian and the other languages using the Cyrillic alphabet. Also Japanese. Also Chinese. *What,* I would wonder in the familiar panic, did I know about the *I Ching?*

I wish I could say this encyclopedic impulse resolved itself in a satisfactory foundation of "enough background." It did not, and it has not. It propelled me forward to become a teacher, the occupation most likely to *intensify* the drive to become encyclopedic. Seeing the ego inflation (after my ego deflation it was a godsend) and the vanity of the drive has moderated and, better still, informed it a little, but encyclopedic puffs still catch my sail unawares, and off I go heading upwind. I am drawn to bookstores as drunks are drawn to dark taverns. Never do I feel more like a drunk than when I am moving observantly through their stacks—PARAPSYCHOLOGY, PARTICLE PHYSICS, POLITICS—practicing restraint.

In my unchartable sprintings and back-treadings

through the wilderness of all possible knowledge, I happened on some bits that held out the promise of organizing the rest. Aided by the patient tuition of one good man, a professor of political philosophy who was unfazed by shrewishness or torpor, I discovered theory. A theory is a symbolic model of what is true. It is simpler than what is true, but it is for that reason an aid to properly aligned thought. All theories pose problems of their own. The best theory points up the most true cases.

The idea of theory is so inherently charming that it is easy to mistake the internal consistency of the theory for the reality it is supposed to suggest. Theories are not true in themselves; they are not stories. I went through a period—the happiest in my encyclopedic quest—in which every theory seemed to be true. This was in part because I so desperately wanted them to be true, in part because the first theories I grasped were so marvelously aligned.

The first was Plato's theory of pure ideas *(eidos),* sometimes translated as "Forms." This was not only perfect in its internal consistency, it corroborated my own feeling that one's experiences were not merely happened upon, nor were they "invented" or "created"; they were *discovered.* But one only discovers what one can recognize, so every discovery requires that one has seen something like it before. Waking discovery is actually an act of deep memory. Our souls are ancient with memory, but they can only remember what is true. Change, movement, history itself is a kind of illusion, an imperfect medium out of which, by training memory, the soul can ascend in eternal communion with what is true. It is a theory of radiant beauty. For Plato the cosmos is a design of enduring harmonies, and mankind has tentatively taken up the lyre.

Plato's cosmology is perfectly, ringingly still. Action, process, growing, dying are all less than real, because what

173

changes is less real than what cannot change. Aristotle, my next theorist, would maintain the perfection, but would forsake the stillness. Aristotle saw an active force, *physis,* driving through all living things, including human communities. This force impels an acorn in the direction of becoming an oak, and a community in the direction of justice. Healthy oaks fulfill the possibilities of oak trees better than stunted oaks do. Just men, whether just carpenters or just kings, fulfill their functions more effectively than unjust ones. Communities are just insofar as their constitutions enable their members to fulfill the functions with which nature has endowed them. There is one *physis* that drives seed into flower, that drives a man to full potential, and that drives a community to flourish in justice. *Physis* is generated from a source, and the source cannot itself be in motion, or generated by any other thing, or it would not *be* the source. Aristotle called the source the Unmoved Mover, or the Uncaused Cause. This too was lovely, with the added loveliness of infusing in-this-world developments with the luster of eternal connectedness.

I did not know how to reconcile Plato's stillness with the relative dynamism of Aristotle. But I was glad for both of them. Their combined thinking seemed to represent a unity more than it did rival claims. I was content to see Aristotle's thought evolving out of Plato's for the sole purpose of sanctifying the living world. So far as I was concerned, Aristotle was not saying, *"This* is the way the truth is revealed," but rather, "This too is the way the truth is revealed." Aristotle is not quite imaginable without Plato, although Plato is imaginable without Aristotle. But I felt better for having them both.

The history of western philosophy is a majestic causeway—at least until the twentieth century where it seems to terminate like the frayed ends of a rope. The philosophers themselves form a gallery of giants: Plato, Aristotle, Augustine, Aquinas, Bacon, Descartes, Spinoza, Hobbes, Locke, Rousseau, Berkeley, Hume, Kant, Hegel, Mill, Marx—. If I were going to paint them, I would enlarge the piazza and insert them into Raphael's *School of Athens*. Ideal Forms, *physis,* nature, reason, history—some unity stands at the center of each magnificent system, and from its fixed sovereignty it orders all the real or seeming variety in creation.

I was especially charmed that Augustine and Aquinas had taken care to align classical thinking with the Jewish and Christian conception of God. This was exactly what I needed. But the more closely acquainted I became with each successive system, the clearer it became—and the more uncomfortable—that philosophy was only apparently a succession. Each system held out the possibility that its model of being was the only one that was true. It occurred to me that philosophy might turn out to be nothing more than an abstract economics in which everything could be plausibly reduced to anything. After all Marx would reduce my quick joy at the flash of an oriole to my father's position in the commercial complex of Chicagoland. Freud would reduce my reverence for the angular beauty of Diana West's face to residual tension accompanying a reawakened infantile drive to have my mother sexually. I had been an undergraduate long enough to know that such claims are plausibly made.

It was no use walking away and saying it is all nonsense: that these elaborate meaning-systems reflect only their creators' dread of meaninglessness. I could not say this because I did not believe it. (I despair for people who do say it, especially those who have been hurt into meaning it.) Until my cocoon, I had had ample, redundant proof of meaning; there had been oracles everywhere. The problem was to find some corroboration in the sphere of thought for what had been so clear to me as a child. For several years beyond

175

college I strove to "unify" philosophy—that is, I scrambled periodically back up into the shafts I had already penetrated and poked around. But I could not do it. I do not have the head for unification. The best I could do was to get the philosophers to seem to argue with each other, and of course everyone argued with Marx. In my classroom I stood by all of them. I claimed that each of the great western philosophers was aiming at some good, that each one had attempted to show the relationship between the waking world and what was eternally true.

And one day after I said just that, it occurred to me that it was true. Realizing this, I realized I could stop carrying around whole philosophical systems in my head like a dozen rattling cages, because the gist of each one was the same: to clarify, to teach, to point to what was good. The systems were *not* about their own elegance; however elegant and big they were, they were out to help. Philosophy was out to do good. Socrates had it right: philosophy is to help us live well. But then they all had it right, except of course Marx. And it was not merely "charming" that Augustine and Acquinas had put the God of ethics and history at the pinnacle of their classicism. So here it was again, this time in thought: God the concept.

The possibility—no, the reality—of God the concept inspired me with hope but at the same time aroused a feeling of inadequacy deeper than I had felt in my wildest bouts of encyclopedism. I did not know much about God the concept, I told myself. I determined to read further. What I liked best was philosophical theology like Whitehead's in which God the concept was safely held at bay inside an elaborate matrix of supporting concepts. For reasons I would not examine I was not eager to encounter God the voice, God the father, and certainly not God the Presence.

But once again God penetrated my (pitiful) defenses

176

through my own teaching. At the time I taught ninth-grade boys an introductory course in western civilization, and for five weeks of the course I would take them though the life and teachings of Jesus.

One day after I had explained, I think, the estimated date of the composition of Matthew's gospel and had said some things appropriate to ninth graders about the oral traditions and the hypothesis that the first three gospels were composed from four sources no longer extant, I began to discuss the Sermon on the Mount, which the boys had read the night before. I don't know precisely when the experience began (I think during the reading of the beatitudes), but for a period of about thirty minutes I felt as if something elemental was thawing out that had been constrictingly frozen in my chest all my life. It was not a specific scriptural passage that caused it, but rather the gentle, yet powerful accretion of so much human force. I wanted to laugh. I wanted to leap up and dance like a maniac. I wanted to beat my chest like a gorilla. I was so happy. *I knew I was such a pompous fool.* But I was outwardly reasonable, a teacher. I said, "You're all probably familiar with this message, but what does it take to 'turn the other cheek'? Has anyone ever tried it? What happens?"

"You probably get belted on the other one."

Exactly, Chip. And what a blessing to be belted cheek after turned cheek for as long as it takes to slap away all your pretensions and pomposity and all your preposterous fear.

This was at once the greatest relief and the greatest joy I had ever known: *I knew what I was afraid of.* I was afraid of every quality (it is one quality) pierced and punctured by Jesus in the sermon. I was afraid of exposure. Since I had first identified myself as a child, I had stopped simply being and had begun the elaborate but hopeless business of creating myself. I had lied repeatedly and stolen to maintain this

177

creation. When it failed to please or when it became too obviously shoddy, I distorted my image of it and blamed others. When it could bear no further exposure, I tried to preserve it in sleep. When I could sleep no longer, I tried to preserve it inside a mountain of knowledge. I had expected knowledge to protect me, not to penetrate my protection. This surprised me because I had not expected knowledge to be *alive;* knowledge, I had assumed, was more like a machine than like an animal. But it was alive, it was more alive than I was. It had now come for me in the form of a man. He was a man into whom everything that is true can be reduced. He had always been there, looking straight into me. It was to shield myself from this look that I had created myself in defense. It was in first turning away from it that my worldly sophistication began. If I do not look at you, I had reasoned, you will not see me.

But here, in a school, in a classroom of boys, I had been found out. I had been penetrated by a text. I was being exposed, and the joy was in letting it happen. I let the words penetrate everything, beginning with the unlikely costume suggesting a scholar of the God concept. There was not really much I would be required to know. Every law, every teaching of the prophets, everything that was or would be true was—was at that moment being—fulfilled by this man. One had only to pay attention and to try. No elaborate offering were necessary, just honest effort. Effort that was conspicuous was very suspect. Prayer need not be elaborate either: acknowledge God, dwell in and acknowledge all present blessings, be generous to others, and use God as a refuge from evil, when you are afraid of it.

The points of prayer were amplified with lessons of perfect simplicity and penetration. If evil's sovereignty is not acknowledged, it is powerless. To return evil is to acknowledge it. Turn the other cheek. Resisting evil and resenting it are also acknowledgments. Give the man your shirt. Carry his burden an extra mile. It is best not to worry about evil's apparently vast dominion, even in a friend or brother or neighbor, for this too is acknowledgment. Where evil is concerned, it is better to tend to oneself, to keep clean, to keep the God-sense vivid, to keep generosity supple. It is easier than anyone imagines for a God-leaning soul to play into the hands of evil. It would be foolish to underestimate the allure of clothes and houses and wealth. One must actively *practice* resisting these things. One must consider the lilies, the birds of the air. They are not, some of them, as miraculous as orioles and tanagers and finches for nothing. I felt wonderful. I was in love again. But this time the object of desire was mine.

Knowing now that I did not have to *do* anything significant in order to matter, I was on fire to do something significant. I wanted to acknowledge God in heaven. I wanted to haul him down to some earthly bandstand and to present him in all his radiance to the public. I wanted to be a bishop, a desert father, to write a new *Bible*. Neighborhoods, lawns, the ivied prospects of the school exuded the soft, loved permanence of Constable's pictures. Everywhere, out of every pane of glass, down every settled walk were es-*sences* again. Life was all story, only story.

I attempted to contain myself. I made an appointment to talk to a teaching friend of mine who was also a priest. This man had a knack. He could offhandedly lend me a book I had been unconsciously screaming for. He made hard work look irresistible.

I told him I needed some advice about some plans I was considering. (I had no plans; all my effort was invested in restraining myself from jumping into the air and whirling my arms about in wide arcs.) As a clergyman, what did he think, I asked, about the relative merits of my becoming ordained

(I was not at the time a member of any church) versus continuing study in theology or ecclesiastical history? (What I wanted to ask was whether one might, under special circumstances, when there was special enthusiasm on the part of the candidate, be made a bishop on the spot.) As my friend's eyes widened in puzzlement, I asked a flurry of questions about denominational practice, about the metaphysical basis of the sacraments. I listened helplessly as I made myself out to be some kind of self-taught spiritual pilot looking for precisely the right ecclesiastical landing strip. I asked the comparative advantages of the world's greatest universities over the world's greatest seminaries. I was speaking animatedly, but I hoped frankly and confessionally, about my aversion to being required to greet and shake hands with strangers in certain church services, when my friend at last spoke.

"You know you don't have to worry about any of these things. You're a Christian."

The instant he said it, I was. I could stop talking at last. I had already realized that an encounter with Christ meant exposure. Sustained exposure would of course mean one's eventual effacement and disappearance; I accepted this in a spirit of good riddance. But each wonder opens onto a field of new wonders. The fact is you do not disappear. Maybe being willing to disappear is enough. I was irrevocably a Christian, and apparently I was easily identifiable as such. And instead of disappearing I had arrived at a condition in which, once again and forever, the stories, including at last mine, came true.

Afterword

My friend the priest advised me to study at Cambridge, and I did. As if through a series of progessively enchanted realms, I departed from Boston, touched down in the gently teeming busyness of London, and boarded a train for Cambridge where I proceeded through a seemingly protective ring of commerce to the university. There, connected in their stones, were the colleges: ecclesiastical cities in patchwork, sure in their spires. This was not a room, but a world of Keats's "casements high and triple arched." The broad backs of the colleges, tended and green, sloped gently to a walled river, still as a canal. Gently arched bridges of worn stone crossed the river at close intervals, and in the perpetual afternoon light of that city, punts glide soundlessly beneath them. At Kings College sheep graze over the green, and swans glide among the punts. I turned off the street, passed into the gates of my college, and entered a dream in which courtyards opened through Gothic archways into more ancient courtyards, each more quiet, more green, more still than the last.

I was formally at the university to study Christian ethics, but I was actually there to confirm my new life through immersion in a new place. (Of course it was a very old life, and a very old place brought it fully to heart.) Cambridge was so deeply permanent that I determined to store it in every cell. All I knew to do was to walk. I could penetrate it, circle around it, gaze up after every ancient prospect. Every day, in all weathers, I passed through old stone arches. I made an ambulatory ritual of entry and departure, of leaving and reentering permanence.

Unknown, really, to anyone there, I walked through the afternoon light of Cambridge. It was a perfect place to give up lingering lies and to walk on, renewed, through every archway. With undiminished surprise and gratitude I realized I was there, in that city, alive, walking. I had given up—and had been given this. And before me, old as the Cambridge stones, settled as the green riverbank, expansive as the tumble of sky over the fens, was the familiar lure of eternity.